WHEN LIFE DOESN'T TURN OUT THE WAY YOU EXPECT

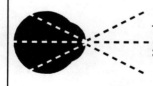

This Large Print Book carries the
Seal of Approval of N.A.V.H.

WHEN LIFE DOESN'T TURN OUT THE WAY YOU EXPECT

MOVING BEYOND . . . DISAPPOINTMENT, REJECTION, BETRAYAL, FAILURE, LOSS

JERRY BRECHEISEN AND LAWRENCE W. WILSON

THORNDIKE PRESS

An imprint of Thomson Gale, a part of The Thomson Corporation

Detroit • New York • San Francisco • New Haven, Conn. • Waterville, Maine • London

THOMSON
GALE

LIBRARY OF CONGRESS CATALOGING-IN-PUBLICATION DATA

Brecheisen, Jerry.
   When life doesn't turn out the way you expect : moving beyond disappointment, rejection, betrayal, failure, loss / by Jerry Brecheisen and Lawrence W. Wilson. — Large print ed.
   p. cm.
   Includes bibliographical references.
   ISBN 0-7862-9062-5 (hardcover : alk. paper)
   1. Suffering — Religious aspects — Christianity. 2. Christian life. 3. Large type books. I. Wilson, Lawrence W., 1959– II. Title.
BT732.7.B692 2006
248.8'6—dc22   2006024206

U.S. Hardcover:
ISBN 13: 978-0-7862-9062-8
ISBN 10: 0-7862-9062-5

Published in 2006 by arrangement with Beacon Hill Press of Kansas City.

Printed in the United States of America on permanent paper
10 9 8 7 6 5 4 3 2 1

CONTENTS

ABOUT THE AUTHORS

Jerry Brecheisen is an author, speaker, and musician who currently serves as Director of Media for his denomination's department of communications. He is the author of 11 books and has edited and compiled numerous other books, manuscripts, and audiovisual scripts. Jerry resides with his wife, Carol, near Indianapolis, Indiana.

Lawrence W. Wilson is managing editor at Wesleyan Publishing House. He has ghost-written, edited, or compiled more than 30 books, and he writes the weekly column "Front Porch" for *The Pendleton Times.* He and his wife, Louisa, live in Anderson, Indiana, with their children, Uriah and Lydia.

PREFACE

It was 10:30 on a drizzly Sunday morning. The charter bus headed east across Kansas on U.S. 40 toward Olathe as an October fog draped itself over the prairie. Gradually at first, almost in slow motion, the tour bus slid on the wet pavement. Before its occupants realized the danger, the massive vehicle was out of control. It crashed violently through the guardrail, toppled over the embankment, and came to rest on its battered side. Most of the 34 passengers were hurled through the broken windows as the bus rolled. Scattered across the wet grass, those who were conscious called out for help.

Nobody heard them.

The day before, these football players from Kansas School for the Deaf, together with coaches, assistants, and cheerleaders, joyously celebrated a 72-12 trouncing of a rival team in Colorado. They had worked

9

together, fought together, triumphed together, not knowing that their lives would soon skid out of control. Even as they reflected on their recent victory, disaster crossed their paths, leaving the wounded crying in pain — unable even to hear their own despairing pleas. Their coach lay dead, unable to come to their aid. Who would hear their cries? Who would help?

Life doesn't always turn out as we've planned. We dream, we dare, and often we achieve. But almost just as often, it seems, life spins out of control. Marriages fail. Bodies succumb to disease. Plans go awry. Friends desert. Children die.

You cry for help. Does anyone hear?

Worse, perhaps, than the trauma itself is the mark it leaves upon the soul. Long after loved ones are buried, wounds are healed, or debts are paid, the marks left by adversity continue to afflict the spirit. Shame, anger, despair, bitterness, remorse, guilt, self-pity — these wounds sometimes remain. Untended, they may never heal. Years later, the faint impression may be seen rising painfully to the surface, affecting our ability to laugh, to love, to live. Physicians aid the body, and counselors treat the mind. But who can heal the broken heart or the crushed spirit?

On the following pages you will meet nine brave souls who bear witness to the fact that God can heal the crushed spirit and the broken heart. Their names and some details of their lives have been changed to guard their privacy, but their stories are real. They are stories — like yours, perhaps — of emotional pain, broken relationships, honest failures, physical disabilities, and heartbreaking guilt. These survivors echo identical messages of hope. Recovery *is* possible. God can heal your heart if you'll let Him.

1
ABUSE
FROM SHAME TO AFFIRMATION

Point of Healing
I accept myself because I know that
God loves me just as I am.

No one can make you feel inferior without
your consent.
— Eleanor Roosevelt

"At first I thought I was imagining it. Nobody could be that cruel. Nobody could be that — sick. Something like that just couldn't happen."

But it did happen.

Stephanie Abrams was 34 years old. Her daughter, Crystal, was 11, the same age Stephanie had been when her mother insisted that she take violin lessons from Mrs. Crandall.

"You can walk to the Crandalls' house after school," her mother had said. "I'll pick you up at five o'clock."

"But, Mom — my lesson is over at 4:15."

"Then I guess you'll have to wait there, won't you? Honestly, Stephanie — try not to be so stupid."

Eloise Crandall was a competent music instructor.

Her husband was a child molester.

"And be nice to Mr. Crandall. I don't want to hear about you acting like a brat."

She knew. My mother knew what was happening — and she still made me go.

"I thought I was losing my mind," Stephanie says. "But one by one, the memories just kept coming back."

Elizabeth Drew, Stephanie's mother, was a beautiful woman whose one desire was to be the object of adoration. Disappointed by life, frightened by her fading beauty, insanely jealous of her daughter, Elizabeth treated Stephanie with all the contempt she felt for herself. She intentionally exposed Stephanie to a known child abuser. She beat both of her children unmercifully, once stabbing Stephanie's brother with a paring knife. She forbade all friendships, insisting that Stephanie walk straight home after school and never visit neighbors.

Every day, in every conversation, with every word and countless actions, Elizabeth

14

Drew bombarded her daughter with the message that would shape Stephanie's self-concept for more than 30 years: *You're fat. You're ugly. You're stupid. You'll never amount to anything.*

"It was a tape that played over and over in my mind," Stephanie explains. "I heard those words from my mother every day of my life."

As an adolescent, Stephanie became a voluntary prisoner in her attic bedroom. "It was the farthest spot in the house from my mother's room," she recalls. She spoke to few children at school. "I knew I was weird; I didn't even try to make friends." She considered suicide. "I hated myself. I hated my life. I had a plan to kill myself, and I would have done it."

Fortunately, when Stephanie was 15, Ronnie Drew finally had enough, and he moved his children out. Stephanie joined a church youth group and began to make friends for the first time in her life. There was even one boy, Mark Abrams, who paid special attention to her. They began dating and soon fell in love. They were married the year after they finished high school. Mark studied accounting at a nearby college, and they began a family. Within a few years, Stephanie all but forgot about the misery of her childhood — until 11-year-old Crystal pointed to the violin case tucked in the back of the closet.

"Mom, did you use to play the violin?"

"Yes, Sweetie, but that was a long time ago."

"I want to take violin lessons, just like you."

And somewhere in Stephanie's mind, somebody pushed "play." *You're fat. You're ugly. You're stupid. You'll never amount to anything. You're fat. You're ugly. You're stupid. You'll never amount to anything.*

THE EFFECT OF ABUSE

Abuse has many forms. Neglect. Incest. Rape. Sexual harassment. Battering. Bullying. Verbal cruelty. And it claims many victims — children, young adults, college students, the elderly, employees, husbands, wives. According to the National Council on Child Abuse and Family Violence, child protective service agencies receive more than 2.5 million reports of child abuse or neglect every year. It's estimated that between one third and one half of all women are physically abused by a male partner at some point in their lives and that five percent of persons over age 65 suffer abuse, usually by a family member.[1]

Victims of abuse come from all social and economic levels, but there's one common feature: at a time when they were helpless, another person harmed them — intentionally. Often the abuser was someone they trusted: a parent, a teacher, an older sibling, a pastor, a relative. The combination of helplessness and betrayal leaves a peculiar scar that can't be seen with the eye. The following are some of its features.

Shame

"I believed her," Stephanie says flatly. "I believed that I was ugly and stupid. I thought there was something wrong with me."

This response is not unusual for victims of abuse. The victims come to believe that they really are wrong or awful or dirty — just as they have been made to feel.

Abuse victims commonly suffer cripplingly low self-esteem. They feel as if a panel of judges is rating them, holding a scorecard with embarrassingly low numbers. Victims often agree with that low assessment of themselves; they would mark the numbers even lower.

False guilt adds to the sense of shame. The abuse victim's mind reasons, "I must

17

be responsible for this somehow." "I must have done something that . . ." "I probably should have . . ."

Sometimes others openly blame the victim for the abuse. "Your Honor, the defendant was known to have dressed in a provocative manner." "How can you accuse my client? These acts were consensual!"

When casual affection becomes inappropriate touching, or when anger gives way to battering, the parting words are always the same: "Don't tell anyone about this." Having suffered emotional or physical trauma by someone they trusted, abuse survivors become wary of entering into other relationships. "I thought nobody could love me," Stephanie says.

Insecurity

Abuse survivors often withdraw socially. They sometimes feel more comfortable being alone than giving or receiving intimacy from another. "If I stay by myself," they reason, "I won't have to face the stares or hear the people talking behind my back." Self-protection is another motive for their withdrawal. "I won't let this happen again!"

Don Marshall entered adolescence with greater-than-usual emotional clumsiness. A camp counselor had invaded his life and left scars. The two were alone in the shower room of the camp swimming pool. The counselor, an older teen, made suggestive comments and then forced the frightened 14-year-old to touch him inappropriately. Don remembers that long walk to the swimming pool. "I felt as if everybody was staring at me. I thought everyone knew." In Don's mind, people were still staring 10 years later. Throughout high school and college, he coped by withdrawing from others.

A public school guidance counselor comments on struggles like the ones Don faced: "Childhood sexual abuse leaves the survivor feeling powerless. Feeling powerless creates conflicting and out-of-control emotions. When a person's most personal and intimate boundaries have been violated, it is natural for him or her to feel he or she has lost control over his or her life."[2] The response? Withdrawal to a safe place.

Perfectionism

Victims sometimes try to avoid further ill-treatment by "being good." Reasoning that there's something wrong with them — something that makes others mistreat them — they aim to be perfect as a shield against further mistreatment. They may even pass this perfectionism on to their children, making unreasonable demands for excellence in order to hide their own inferiority behind the child's achievement.

Mary Adams is in counseling for her obsessive-compulsive behavior. After several months of therapy, she came to see a link between her three and four showers every day and the first time she was forced by her stepbrother to watch pornographic movies and submit to his touches. Her response? Try to be perfect. "I had to dust every figurine on the fireplace mantle — every day," she adds. "I can't even remember how many times I've washed and rewashed clothing and bedding." It became a strange yet acceptable way of life. She tried to hide her feelings of inadequacy behind her patterned behavior.

Steve Reynolds doesn't know how many times he's been to confession. But he remembers that it was always for the same thing: that afternoon when his mother, the one he trusted most, betrayed him by manipulating his emotions. She had used the rejection of her husband to gain her son's sympathy — and then to entice him. "Honor your father and your mother." The words rang like a bell in his head. But there was a silence in his heart that a thousand celebrations of mass did not fill.

He thought that if he became an altar boy, if he went to seminary, if he took a vow of celibacy — if he could just be *good* enough — the bad could be erased. But no amount of good behavior could wash away the shame he felt.

Anger

Anger is a natural response to injustice, and most victims of abuse feel it. Since their suffering is often secret, however, it's difficult to deal with their anger openly. In some cases, that anger turns to violence. Every year, more than 3 million children witness domestic violence. And every year approximately 4,000 American women are killed by their spouses or boyfriends.[3] Much of that violence is perpetrated by victims of abuse. Anger becomes a means of coping, a way of acting out the injustice that's felt in the soul. The cycle continues.

Not all who are abused become abusers. But most feel anger and must cope with it. "I screamed. I threw dishes. I literally terrified Mark and Crystal," Stephanie admits.

Depression

Anger turned inward may become depression. Abuse — physical, emotional, or sexual — burdens the victim with memories that cannot be changed. The once-vibrant spirit is drained of energy. Helplessness gives birth to hopelessness. The blows, the angry words, or forced intimacy did more damage than imagined. The cup of life now seems half empty rather than half full.

I hate the holidays, Sheila Robertson thought. *It's been two years, and it still makes me cringe.* Her low mood wasn't caused by the stress of shopping or entertaining. It came from the day her fiancé exploded over the purchase of a Christmas tree. He told her that he had something special for her — it was a blackened eye and bruised ribs. Now the smell of evergreen almost made her sick.

She's not alone. For victims of abuse, the times that should be the most joyous are often the most painful. Holidays, birthdays, graduations, and vacations become painful reminders of "what happened." Special occasions become special reminders of the past they cannot change.

Those who have suffered abuse — and those who have known and loved them — realize the powerful effect on the human spirit. The scars are deep. Abuse wounds its victims in profound ways, but the scars can be healed. God's Word is candid about the depravity of human behavior and its devastating effects. It is equally forthright about the power of grace and the miraculous healing it can bring. Scripture contains a message of hope for the abused.

GOD'S WORD

The Bible is more than a book of theology or law. It's also a sweeping history of God and His people. The saga is filled with engaging tales of heroism and courage. And it depicts the worst of human behavior — treachery, betrayal, and even abuse. Among the saddest stories in Scripture is that of Tamar, the daughter of King David. It's recorded in 2 Sam. 13.

Tamar's Story

Tamar was a beautiful young woman, sister of Absalom, one of David's most promising sons. David had many children by his several wives. One of his sons, Amnon, became first attracted to and then obsessed with the beauty of his half-sister Tamar. Although it would have been possible in those days for Amnon to marry her, he wanted only to use her for his own pleasure. Pretending to be ill, he sent word that he would feel better if only Tamar would come and take care of him by preparing a meal and serving it to him in his private quarters.

23

When Tamar arrived, Amnon sent everyone else out of the room and then brazenly invited her to have sex with him. She refused. He made advances on her. She begged him to stop, but he would not listen. Finally, he overpowered her and raped her.

Then, as happens so often in cases of abuse, Amnon turned his own shame upon Tamar. "Get out!" he screamed at her.

Tamar was petrified. She realized that she had been raped but now feared the public humiliation that would accompany Amnon's treatment of her. Knowing that in their culture the only way to avoid public shame was to marry Amnon, Tamar refused to leave. She pleaded with Amnon to marry her and avoid the disgrace that would surely follow both of them — Amnon for having raped her, her for having had sex before marriage. Amnon refused. Calling for his servant, he had Tamar thrown out of his house.

Hurled into the street in front of her brother's house, Tamar began wailing aloud. She fled through the streets of Jerusalem to the home of her brother Absalom. Tearing off her elegant gown, Tamar dressed herself in rags and covered herself with ashes as a sign of sorrow. Absalom tried to console her, but she was beyond consolation. Abuse had left a deep scar. Shame and anger became the guiding emotions of her life. The last words that the Bible records about Tamar form a picture of utter despair: "And Tamar lived in her brother Absalom's house, a desolate woman" (2 Sam. 13:20).

Shame turned the ravishingly beautiful princess into a bitter and broken woman. Bitterness turned the daughter of a king into a despondent recluse. Tamar was a victim — not only of rape but also of a far subtler cruelty: self-pity. Unable to free herself from the shame of what another had done, she allowed anger to poison every relationship in her life.

Two years later, Absalom murdered his half-brother Amnon in revenge for the rape of his sister.

For those who have suffered abuse, the first priority is to get free from the abuser. But physical freedom does not bring release from chains that bind the soul. Years after the threat of imminent harm has been removed, shame, anger, and other damaging effects may continue. Like Tamar, victims of abuse often accept the victimizer's judgment of themselves: "You're worthless — now get out!"

Tamar's story has a sad ending. But many victims of abuse are able to overcome their abuse. Healing *is* possible. There's a way to remove the burden of false shame and all that goes with it. That happens when one comes to feel genuine affirmation, the only affirmation that really matters: acceptance by God.

The Woman Caught in Adultery

Tamar's story has a rough counterpart in the New Testament. The incidents do not form an exact parallel, but they both center upon women who were made victims of someone else's desire. Whereas one depicts the power of shame, the other reveals the power of acceptance. The event is recorded in John 8:2–11 and involves an unnamed woman caught in the most humiliating of circumstances.

Jesus was teaching a group of people at the Temple one day when some lawyers and religious leaders shoved their way to the front, dragging with them a woman who had been caught in the act of adultery. Their purpose was to embarrass Jesus with a difficult legal and moral question. To do so, they publicly shamed this woman, forcing her to stand — perhaps only partly clothed — in front of the crowd and broadcast to the world what she had done. Since adultery was technically a capital offense in those days, they asked Jesus what He thought they should do with her. They were unconcerned with the woman herself and probably cared little about the fact that she had committed adultery. They were using her to advance their own purpose — to embarrass Jesus with a difficult question.

Although the woman (unlike Tamar) was actually guilty of something, Jesus ignored that fact, stooping to write some words in the dust with His finger. No one knows what He wrote, but the words had a powerful effect. One by one, the lawyers and hypocrites who had exposed this woman to shame walked silently away.

"Where are they?" Jesus asked her. "Is anyone accusing you now?"

"No one," she answered.

"Then neither do I," Jesus said, adding the admonition to leave her sinful lifestyle behind.

Like so many others whom Jesus met, this woman discovered that there is a powerful antidote to the disease of shame — acceptance. This is the miracle of God's grace: He loves you just as you are. Nothing you have done — and nothing that has been done *to* you — causes God to see you as unlovely or unlovable. He loves and accepts you just as you are.

When we accept the judgment of others about us, we feel shamed. Tamar accepted Amnon's vision of her — unacceptable, unwanted, worthless. Stephanie accepted her mother's vision of her — fat, ugly, stupid. But the anonymous woman caught in adultery listened to a different voice — the voice of God. Jesus accepted her. Jesus loved her. Jesus set her free. When we accept God's opinion of us, we're released from the prison of shame that claims us all, especially victims of abuse. God loves you. He sees you as a beautiful, likable, lovely person. And like a painter, putting the finishing touches on a portrait masterpiece, He adds strokes of grace to your life.

Come into His studio. Be still. Just watch. Your portrait is on the canvas. Someone has marred it. Ugly blotches distort your image. "Father," you dare call Him. "Can You do anything with it?"

He picks up the palate of grace and walks to the easel that holds your damaged image. You watch as He lifts the brush to the canvas. The master speaks aloud as He works.

"Here's what you need — a little brightening. I'll just add some white."

Shadows disappear beneath the firm, careful strokes. A new image takes shape, an image of wholeness and healing. The master has painted a new picture of you — a picture of beauty, a picture of purpose, a picture of worth.

For that's what you truly are: Beautiful. Valuable. Lovable.

STEPS TO HEALING

You stand in awe of the masterpiece. *Can that beautiful person really be me?* It is. As you wrap your new portrait and take it out of the studio into the world, you realize there will be challenges. Accepting God's view of you is the starting point. Acting upon that new vision of reality must come next — and that's not easy. In the real world of family pressures, work stresses, and haunting memories, will you be able to hold on to the vision of yourself that God has given you?

Here are some steps that may help on your road to healing — a road map left by other travelers who have made the journey from shame to acceptance.

Refuse the Blame

Shame is a destructive force. In fact, it's one of Satan's chief weapons in the war for your soul. He is called *the accuser,* and with good reason. In cases of abuse, the wrong person usually feels the shame. Victimizers are adept at rationalizing their behavior. "She flirted with me." "He had it coming." "She knew I was going to be angry."

Oddly, it's the victim who often feels responsible for being abused. "I shouldn't have been nice to him." "It's my fault for talking back." "I must have said the wrong thing."

Refuse to accept the blame for things you did not do. You're not responsible for what was done *to* you.

Cling to God's Word

It's important that you not believe what you see on television. In that world, everyone is handsome, witty, intelligent, sexy, and successful — not to mention thin. Popular media bombard us with false images of life. Don't believe them.

God's Word tells us the truth about ourselves — we're forgiven, we're loved, and we're free. Search the Scriptures for God's promises of acceptance, and then cling to them with all your might. Let the Word be your rock.

Tell the Truth

More than 30 years after she suffered the abuse from her mother, Stephanie Abrams told her father the truth. "God told me to do it," she says. "I tried to resist, but it's hard to say no to God." Stephanie's dad had never known the full extent of the abuse she and her brother had endured. She believed that her silence shielded him from unnecessary anguish. But after 30 years, it was time for the truth to come out.

While there may be no value in making private things public, it's often helpful to the victims of abuse to acknowledge the truth — first to themselves, then to others who can offer support. Talking to a parent, a friend, or a counselor can be an important step to healing.

That step is essential if abuse is still taking place. If you're now being abused, *tell someone.*

Look to the Future

Tamar's answer to abuse was to hide in the home of her brother. Privacy is important, but isolation is dangerous. There can be no healing until the victim makes the determination to face and resolve the issue. Don't ignore or minimize the problem. Don't isolate yourself. Seek comfort and advice. Make the decision to move forward.

"You have to make a choice," Stephanie says. "You can decide to let this thing ruin your life, or you can decide to let God make something of it."

Will the past determine your future? Will you be chained in a prison of fear? Or will you choose to move forward? Will you make friends, continue your education, date again?

Choose the future. There are no possibilities in the past.

Listen for the Voice of God

G. Campbell Morgan said, "I believe in the promises of God enough to venture an eternity on them." Listening for those promises is vital for spiritual healing. God speaks in many different ways. He can speak through the Bible, the Holy Spirit, sermons, Christian radio and television, worship, or Christian music.

"God may not come in through your front door," says Stephanie. "You have to read the Bible, get to church, and listen for His voice."

In what ways do you seek God's voice? If He speaks to you, will you be listening?

Work While You Wait

Your healing may not be instantaneous. Healing seldom is. Your recovery will take time — so let it. In the meantime, get to work. Ministry is good therapy. Ask God what you can do that will be a help to others. It might be something as simple as tending the yard for a neighbor, or it could be something as challenging as sharing your story with another survivor. God has a job for you, something you can do to glorify His name. So find it and do it.

THE POINT OF HEALING

The kitchen was strewn with shattered dishes. Crystal screamed hysterically as Mark Abrams clutched her to his chest and paced slowly toward the door. Stephanie stood in the center of the chaotic scene, her hands trembling, tears streaming from her eyes. Anger and anxiety over her stolen childhood had reached an explosive level, and her behavior had become erratic.

"I'm taking Crystal to my mother," Mark said slowly. "When I come back, we're going to decide what to do. I'm not going to live like this anymore."

That day became the catalyst for change in Stephanie's life. Recognizing that the pain of her past now jeopardized her future, she began a series of steps that led to her healing.

A nominal Christian until that point, Stephanie renewed her relationship with

God. Prayer and Bible reading suddenly became important to her — especially God's promises of acceptance. "I lived on Scripture," she recalls. "I'm amazed at the number of times God has spoken to me through this Book." She also began seeing a counselor, who helped her to accept herself and gain a new sense of worth. Best of all, among the many memories that Stephanie recovered, some were affirming, and one became her spiritual touchstone.

At 16 years of age, Stephanie stayed at a friend's over Christmas. Short of beds but long on hospitality, the Carlsons had prepared a cot for Stephanie in the living room next to the Christmas tree. Although she was happy to enjoy the season with a stable family, Stephanie couldn't help but notice the contrast to her own life. She went to sleep with her mother's demeaning accusations playing over and again in her mind.

The next morning, Mrs. Carlson rose early to make breakfast for the family, and Stephanie woke as the good-hearted woman passed through the living room.

Mrs. Carlson stopped, sat on the edge of the cot, and rested a hand on Stephanie's shoulder. "What a lovely surprise to find you under my Christmas tree!" she said, smiling thoughtfully. "You're the best

Christmas present anybody could have."

To this day, tears well in Stephanie's eyes as she remembers that scene. "I couldn't believe anyone could ever feel that way about me," she says. "I treasure those words, and I've come to believe them."

Child of God, you — *you* — are a precious gift. Your life matters to God. He loves you, and He wants you. You are precious in His sight. Believe those words and treasure them: you are the best present anyone could ever have.

YOUR JOURNEY

Exploring Your Story

1. In what ways is your story like Stephanie's? In what ways is it different?

2. How do you tend to react when you feel helpless?

3. Do you ever feel shame because of what other people think of you?

Exploring God's Word

1. Read the story of Tamar in 2 Sam. 13. Who behaved well? Who behaved badly?

2. Read John 8:2−11. Why do you think Jesus reacted to this situation the way He did?

3. If Jesus said something right now to

Tamar — or to you — what do you think it would be?

Exploring the Steps to Healing

1. Make a list of affirming things people have said to you. Add to the list the things you know about yourself based on God's Word.

2. Is there anyone you need to tell concerning what happened (or is happening) to you?

3. Spend some time praying today, asking God what ministry or service you can do to help someone else.

2
BETRAYAL
FROM ANGER TO FORGIVENESS

Point of Healing
I will forgive others because God has forgiven me.

To lick your wounds, to smack your lips over grievances long past, to roll over your tongue the prospect of bitter confrontations still to come, to savor to the last toothsome morsel both the pain you are given and the pain you are giving back — in many ways it is a feast fit for a king. The chief drawback is that what you are wolfing down is yourself. The skeleton at the feast is you.
— Frederick Buechner

"What's wrong with this thing? I can't get on the Internet!" Ron Weiss called out angrily from the spare room of his Marion, Ohio, home. "I have a business meeting in less than an hour. I can't deal with this right now."

That's odd, thought Sandy, his wife of 23 years. *I was using the computer earlier with no problems.* After the successful realtor left for an appointment across town, Sandy thought she would try to help. Her husband had given her his password several weeks earlier when another computer problem had come up. She signed on to investigate.

Almost immediately, she wished she hadn't.

Noticing that the first dozen or so E-mail messages had the same screen name, Sandy wondered if the computer might have a virus. She opened the first message and was horrified at what she read. It contained two or three paragraphs addressed to Ron, filled with sexually explicit language. More shocking was the closing line. After the words "Til tonight, my darling" was the name of Sandy's best friend.

"I was in shock," Sandy remembers. "I sat there staring at the screen for what seemed like an hour."

How could she? How could he?

"At first I was puzzled, then stunned. Then I just got mad."

Twenty-three years of marriage. . . . I trusted him. I loved him. We have four daughters who think the sun rises and sets on him.

For some time, Sandy had known that there were problems in her marriage. Several months earlier she had begged Ron to go with her to see their pastor.

"I don't have a problem," he replied smugly. "Maybe *you* ought to go see him."

Sandy did exactly that. The pastor listened carefully, shared some Scripture, and prayed with her. "I felt much better after that," she said, "and things did get better for a while."

Now this!

"I was devastated," Sandy recalls. "The fact that I'd been working so hard to improve our marriage made it even worse."

That night when Ron arrived home near midnight, Sandy pretended to be asleep. She lay there silently awake, seething with anger, as he got into bed.

The next morning Sandy feigned normalcy as she stirred eggs to make omelets and breathed the aroma of fresh coffee.

"I'm going to the fitness center after I drop the girls off at volleyball practice," Ron said as he helped Sandy clear the table.

Sandy resented his cheerfulness. She snapped, "Ron, we have to talk."

"Now?"

"No, after you drop the girls off."

Later, they sat in the sunshine on their

new deck. "I know about the affair," she said curtly.

Ron faked a counter "What are you talking about?"

"When you said you were having trouble getting on the Net, I tried to help."

Her husband's face was ashen. "Sandy, it's not what you think. It — it just got out of hand. Honey, I'm so sorry."

"It's too late for that, Ron. I want you out of my house before the girls get home."

"What will I do? Where will I go?"

Sandy's anger flared. "You should have thought of that a long time ago," she said, and she walked quickly into the bedroom and slammed the door.

The postbetrayal days were a waking nightmare, shuffling through the routines of work and home. There were trips to the doctor. "He put me on antidepressants." And phone calls to the lawyer. "We'll need $2,000 to get started on the divorce." Her life became a blur of depression and anxiety. "But mostly I was angry. I gave that man my whole life — and he lied to me. But even so, I was confused. I didn't know what to do."

THE EFFECT OF BETRAYAL
Any human relationship can be broken by

betrayal. Sandy experienced a betrayal of the most intimate kind — by a spouse. She was violated at a second level — by her friend. Someone she had considered a confidante, almost a sister, violated her trust. From playground pals to college roommates to spouses to business partners to siblings to friends — all who entrust themselves to another human being are susceptible to betrayal.

When the rules of life change, what's right? Who do you trust? Fear and suspicion become the new rules of engagement in life's war. The effects are devastating.

Anger

Anger follows betrayal as surely as thunder follows lightning. From the instant you realize that trust has been broken, the seed of anger begins to sprout. Some symptoms of anger are obvious, others less so. The deepest hurts lie deep in the heart. You remember the intimate talks late at night, the assurances for the future, the promises.

The writer of Hebrews warned, "See to it that no one misses the grace of God and that no bitter root grows up to cause trouble and defile many" (Heb. 12:15). For those who have known betrayal, anger can become an entangling vine.

Aggression

A cornered animal bares its teeth, preparing to fight. Its safety compromised, desperate to defend its offspring, it lashes out violently. Outdoorsmen will tell you that there is no more dangerous animal than a mother bear protecting her cubs.

That instinct to defend, so common in nature, exists in human beings also. Lashing out at the betrayer or suspected accomplices is a way of defending turf, ensuring the safety of home, children, career, or finances. When threatened, normally genteel people may turn into warriors. "I'll sue them for everything they're worth!" "I'm filing a grievance with the ethics board. I'll take her license away." "Let me get in the same room with him. We'll settle this thing the hard way."

"This isn't like you," friends will say. "I've never seen you like this." *Of course not! Nobody's ever stabbed me in the back before.* It will take a supernatural change to keep the hunted from becoming the hunter, a change of heart that only God can bring.

Vengeance

The ultimate fruit of anger and aggression is vengeance — the desire to harm the betrayer. Disguised as a hunger for justice, this brand of hatred seeks to legitimize itself in our minds. *It's only right. I'll make them pay for what they've done.*

The true motive is usually obvious, even to the victim of betrayal. "I was so angry I wanted to strangle him," Sandy admits of the days following the revelation of Ron's affair. "I wanted to hurt him — just like he hurt me."

Grief

Something dies in a betrayal. Innocence. Naiveté. Relationship. Love. Hope. Trust that was built over months or years is crushed. Dreams succumb to disappointment.

That death is followed by mourning, often including the same painful process that accompanies the loss of a loved one to sudden death. "I was a mess," Sandy recalls. "I went back and forth between being angry and sad. I cried all the time."

Denial. Anger. Depression. Bargaining. These are the familiar stages of grief, and they accompany betrayal as well. There may be no casket or gravesite, but betrayal leaves an empty place in the heart — or an empty chair at the table. There may even be a wake of sorts as friends gather to share sympathy and tears. Soon everyone else returns to their "normal lives." But the betrayed one, like a grieving widow or widower, is left alone.

GOD'S WORD

Not all of God's people are perfect angels. Some of them, in fact, behave quite badly from time to time. The Bible tells the story of many individuals, God's chosen people, who appeared to be playing for the other team. One of them was Jacob.

Jacob was one of twin sons born to Isaac and Rebekah. As the younger child, he missed by a whisker inheriting a fortune from his father — and the promise of divine blessing that went with it. Older brother Esau would inherit the title. Jacob would have to work for a living.

But work of the manual kind didn't suit Jacob. He preferred to live by his wits, and for the next 40 years he worked a con on everyone he met, trying to hustle his way to the good life that he had missed out on at birth.

Jacob's first and greatest con was when he cheated his brother, Esau, out of his inheritance. It's a story of treachery, betrayal, and hatred; and, ultimately, it's a story of reconciliation. You can read it in the Book of Genesis, chapters 27 through 33.

Esau and Jacob

Esau and Jacob were twins, but they were about as identical as a wolverine and a toy poodle. Predictably, they didn't always get along. Their sibling rivalry started even before birth: their mother Rebekah felt them jostling each other within her womb. When big brother Esau came forth in the world, little brother Jacob came right behind him, grasping at his heel. And that's the way they lived — Jacob always trying to get ahead of Esau.

Esau grew into an outdoorsman. Like his father, Isaac, he loved to hunt. Jacob took after his mother's side of the family and favored intellectual pursuits. He was always thinking, always planning, always plotting ways to get ahead. By law, Esau would inherit his father's property; he was the oldest son. But remember that Isaac was the son of Abraham, to whom God had made great promises. Abraham, through his descendants, would become the father of a great nation. Esau stood to receive that blessing as well. He was destined for greatness.

One day Esau came in from a hunting expedition that had gone poorly. He had had no luck and had nearly exhausted himself. Not having the sharpest of minds,

Esau exaggerated his situation, believing himself to be on the verge of death. "Give me some of that stew you're making," Esau begged his brother, "and I'll give you anything you want."

Jacob saw his opportunity and seized it. "I'll swap it for your birthright," he offered.

It was a sucker's trade. Esau stood to inherit all that his father had. Would he trade that for a bowl of soup? Did he think Jacob was serious? Did he really believe he was that close to starvation after only a day or two of going without food? We'll never know the answers to those questions, but we do know this: Esau agreed. He allowed his brother to swindle him out of his most valuable possession.

Time went by, and perhaps Esau forgot about the ridiculous bargain he had made. But Jacob didn't. Jacob was not home free yet. He still had to convince his father to settle the firstborn rights upon him. Isaac was old but not a fool. He would never uphold the preposterous deal his sons had made.

That's when Rebekah entered the picture. Favoring Jacob shamelessly, she conspired with him to trick the nearly blind Isaac. Dressing Jacob up in hunting clothes and disguising his soft skin with an animal hide, she sent him to his father. Pretending to be Esau, Jacob asked for the old man's blessing. Isaac was skeptical, but he finally agreed. He blessed Jacob, conferring upon him all the privileges of the firstborn.

At that very moment, Esau arrived.

Esau was enraged, as was Isaac, but there was nothing to be done. Once given, the blessing could not be retracted. It was legally binding. Both men realized that Jacob had deceived them. Esau ranted and stormed and finally broke down weeping like a child. Everything he possessed was lost — stolen by his own brother.

Esau's anger soon turned to hatred. He respected his father enough to let the matter rest during his lifetime, but Esau privately vowed to kill Jacob as soon as Isaac was dead. Rebekah, fearing for Jacob's life, warned him of the plot, and Jacob ran away.

For years the two men lived separately. Jacob fled to the home of his uncle Laban, worked for him, and eventually married two of his daughters. He spent many years building a family and wrangling with Laban, perhaps the only man more shrewd than himself.

After a series of business arrangements that always seemed to favor Jacob, Laban suspected that he was being cheated. The two men had a falling out, and Jacob decided to get out while the getting was good. But where could he go? Back home, where he would be at the mercy of Esau? Jacob determined to risk his fate at Esau's hands and packed his family, by now quite numerous, and his possessions, an abundance of livestock and goods, and headed home.

What reception would he receive? Had the years abated Esau's fury? He had vowed to kill Jacob; would he now make good that threat? As he grew nearer home, Jacob knew that his life was in danger. Adding to his fear was a report that Esau was headed to meet him — accompanied by 400 men! The next day the two brothers would meet for the first time in 20 years. Fearing for his life, Jacob sent lavish gifts of livestock ahead, hoping to appease his brother. Then he went along himself, the betrayer now at the mercy of his victim.

At midday the two of them met on the road. There was Jacob with all the wealth he had gained. Would Esau believe it should all be his? Esau was there, along with his 400 men. Would he finally take vengeance on the brother who had betrayed him?

As they approached one another, Jacob bowed to the ground seven times before his brother. But Esau ran to meet Jacob and embraced him. He threw his arms around Jacob's neck and kissed him, and they both wept. Esau had forgiven his brother. The two were reconciled.

The Bible says little about the reason for Esau's change of heart. It's obvious, though, that something dramatic had happened. His heart had softened toward his brother. Hatred was replaced by a loving embrace; threats of revenge gave way to tears. The two were reconciled. A miracle had taken place in Esau's heart — the miracle called forgiveness.

STEPS TO HEALING

To forgive is decidedly unnatural, and there's nothing easy about it. Anger and resentment are difficult weeds to pull. Trust is difficult to build in the first place and is humanly almost impossible to rebuild. Yet it *is* possible to forgive. In fact, it's a *requirement* for maintaining spiritual health. We can't be truly whole, at peace, and spiritually strong until we learn to do this thing that seems so difficult for human beings to do.

By what means is grace applied to the wound of betrayal? How does the change of heart called forgiveness come about? Here are some practical steps that lead from

49

anger to grace.

Acknowledge Anger Appropriately

Esau initially had the right idea, but he pursued it in the wrong way. He was angry about what his brother had done. And who can blame him? Jacob took advantage of his brother, deceived his father, and won by treachery something he was not entitled to. That was terribly wrong, of course. But Esau's vow of revenge was also wrong. His anger — as it often does in the victim of betrayal — turned to something ugly and selfish called vengeance.

There's nothing Christian about denying anger. Anger is a real emotion and is a natural response to injustice. We do ourselves no favor by pretending not to be angry when wronged. Yet processing anger appropriately is the challenge. One way to acknowledge anger while steering clear of vengeance is to include yourself in the family of sinners. It is, after all, a heritage we all share, even though when we become Christians we put our sinful lives behind us. Both betrayer and victim are guilty in God's eyes, albeit for separate offenses. When you recall the fact that you, too, have sinned, perhaps even betraying the trust of others, it helps prevent reasonable expressions of anger from growing to destructive thoughts. Paul reminds us to "bear with each other and forgive whatever grievances you may have against one another. Forgive as the Lord forgave you" (Col. 3:13).

It may take years to fully express your anger and release it. But it will never happen at all if you don't begin. In "A Poison Tree," William Blake writes

I was angry with my friend:
I told my wrath, my wrath did end.
I was angry with my foe:
I told it not, my wrath did grow.

Theologian Paul Tillich said that forgiveness is remembering the past in order to forget it. Find ways to acknowledge the injustice that's been done to you without resorting to injustice yourself.

Let the Anger Go
Following the 1981 release of the American hostages seized at the United States Embassy and held prisoner in Iran, President Ronald Reagan offered them a piece of good advice. "Turn the page," he told them, advising them to let go of the past and work on building their futures. That's still good advice.

Lingering on the wounds of the past is self-defeating. At some point, one must say "Enough." Anger is hot, like a radioactive metal. In small amounts, radiation is helpful — in X-rays, for example. When held too long, however, it becomes lethal. So it is with anger. It can be the spark that lights the fire of justice. But held too long, it becomes something harmful called revenge. In time, our anger ceases to be productive and becomes self-destructive. Will Rogers said, "People who fly off into a rage always make a bad landing." We harm ourselves, not others, when we seek revenge, bear grudges, and nurse hatred.

Use your anger to motivate your search for truth and justice. Then let it go.

Admit That You Must Forgive

"Close the door after me" is a sentiment often expressed by those seeking privilege. "Let me build a house near this pristine mountain lake — then bar any further development."

Forgiveness-seekers often feel the same. "Lord, forgive me for my sins — but punish my enemies for theirs!" We hoard forgiveness, as we do so many other possessions, enjoying for ourselves what we deny to others.

Jesus doesn't allow it.

In one of the more unsettling lines from His Sermon on the Mount, Jesus unequivocally tied our own forgiveness by God to our willingness to forgive others. He said, "If you forgive men when they sin against you, your heavenly Father will also forgive you. But if you do not forgive men their sins, your Father will not forgive your sins" (Matt. 6:14–15).

Forgiveness matters. We do not have the option to withhold it from others; we are required to forgive. That sounds harsher than it is. Jesus had our own good in mind when He urged us to forgive. Saying that those who have been wronged are required to forgive is like saying those who have had surgery must do physical therapy. Anyone who has had physical therapy knows that it's grueling and painful. It hurts almost as much as the surgery. But total healing will not take place without it.

Forgiveness is similar. It hurts. But it's absolutely necessary to forgive others if our own hearts are to be healed.

Attempt Realistic Reconciliation

Jacob and Esau were tearfully reunited after years of living in animosity. It was a beautiful scene of reconciliation. Is that possible for you?

Perhaps it is. Broken marriages are often restored. Parents and children who have not spoken to one another for years are sometimes happily reunited. Old enemies occasionally join hands in friendship. One of the most beautiful things God does is to restore something that was broken, putting it back the way it was. That, in fact, is what the gospel is all about.

Is it possible that you might be reconciled with the one who has betrayed you? Have you released your anger so that you can forgive? Has the other party acknowledged his or her fault and sought forgiveness? Perhaps you, like Esau, may have the opportunity to be reunited with one whom you once loved. The apostle Paul told first-century Christians that when it came to forgiveness, the ball was always in their court: "If it is possible, as far as it depends on you, live at peace with everyone" (Rom. 12:18).

But sometimes the gap is so great that it isn't possible to be reconciled. And reconciliation doesn't always lead to restoration. After Jacob and Esau were reunited, the effects of Jacob's betrayal were not reversed. He continued to hold the superior position in the family, and the two chose not to settle near one another. Not every broken relationship will be repaired, but forgiveness is still possible. In fact, it's a requirement that must be met in order to facilitate your own healing.

Let God Do It

Forgiveness is not something you can do on your own. There is no 1-2-3 formula, no six simple steps. Forgiveness depends on the miracle of grace, and you need God's help.

Corrie ten Boom, the Holocaust survivor who became a "tramp for the Lord," well known for her extensive itinerant ministry, made this discovery one day when she came face to face with a former S.S. guard from Ravensbruk, the concentration camp where she was interred during World War II.

Corrie had spoken in a church on the subject of grace. After the service, a man approached her and said, "How grateful I am for your message, *Fräulein!* To think that, as you say, [God] has washed my sins away!" She recognized the man instantly as one of her former captors. Her mind was flooded with pain, humiliation, and anger. The man extended his hand to shake hers, but Corrie kept her hand at her side.

"Even as the angry, vengeful thoughts

boiled through me," she later said, "I saw the sin of them. Jesus Christ had died for this man; was I going to ask for more? 'Lord Jesus,' I prayed, 'forgive me, and help me to forgive him.' " Still, she could not extend her hand to this man, a former S.S. guard. "Jesus," she prayed again, "I cannot forgive him. Give me Your forgiveness." And then she shook his hand.

At that moment a miracle took place. Corrie relates, "From my shoulder along my arm and through my hand a current seemed to pass from me to him, while into my heart sprang a love for this stranger that almost overwhelmed me." She concludes, "When God tells us to love our enemies, he gives, along with the command, the love itself."[1]

If you think you can't forgive the one who hurt you, you're right. *But God can.* Let Him do it through you.

THE POINT OF HEALING

Sandy and Ron divorced two years after the affair. "We did try to reconcile," she says, "but it wasn't possible. Ron had worse problems than I knew." Sandy later learned — from her daughter — of her husband's serial infidelity. The affair had not been an isolated incident. Her daughter's boyfriend had seen him with another woman the year before, and her daughter, Cheri, knew about two other affairs.

"I didn't want to hurt you," Cheri explained.

"But the hurt didn't stop," Sandy relates. "It hurts today, almost as much as it did five years ago, but the blame left — and the anger."

Blame and anger had become Sandy's constant companions. Scheming for revenge, belittling Ron to his children, looking for ways to shame him to others — Sandy did all those things in the months following the affair. Every day was filled with bitter thoughts.

Without realizing it, she made herself a prisoner of her own resentment. "I became a bitter, lonely person," she laments.

The turning point came at 7:30 one Monday morning. Sandy drove to work in tears, recalling the devastated, angry feeling of discovering Ron's E-mail. She sat in the parking lot, hunched over the steering wheel, sobbing. "I was trying to decide whether I should try to go to work or just go home. I don't know if it was God's voice I heard or if I just finally realized the truth, but that's the moment it dawned on me — Ron wasn't hurting me anymore. I was hurting myself."

After the divorce, Ron's presence was minimized in Sandy's life. The children were coping reasonably well. "It was me who was keeping the affair alive," Sandy admits. "I knew that I needed to forgive him if I was ever going to be free."

What followed were months of conversations with a close friend, a round of counseling appointments, and lots of prayer. Sandy says, "It started that day in the parking lot. That's the day I chose to forgive Ron for what he did to me."

Sandy discovered the power of choice in her healing. It was an act of her will that led to a change in her heart.

Impossible?

Ask Esau. Miracles do happen.

"Father, forgive them," Jesus prayed as He hung from the Cross He never deserved as those to whom He had shown only love showed anger, "for they do not know what they are doing" (Luke 23:34). The road to healing begins with those words.

Are you ready to say them?

Your Journey

Exploring Your Story

1. In what ways is your story the same as Sandy's? How is it different?

2. Which effect of betrayal has been most prominent in your heart — grief or anger? Why do you think that's so?

3. Betrayal seldom involves just one person. Make a list of the people in your situation who let you down, and describe your current feelings toward them.

Exploring God's Word

1. In what ways might Esau's life have been different if his brother had not betrayed him? In what ways was it the same, with or without his birthright?

2. Why do you think Esau forgave his brother? How do you think he might have arrived at that decision?

3. Do a brief study on the concept of forgiveness in the New Testament. List four or five discoveries you make about it, and share them with someone.

Exploring the Steps to Healing

1. Name some things you have done in response to your anger. Which of them have been healthy, and which have been unhealthy?

2. If you were to be reconciled to those who betrayed you, what would you have to change in you? What would have to change in them?

3. What is the next step you need to take in order to achieve spiritual wholeness? Are you willing to take that step? If not, why not?

3
Loss
FROM DESPAIR TO HOPE

Point of Healing
I believe that with God,
the future will be better than the past.

Parting is all we know of heaven,
And all we need of hell.
                                    — Emily Dickinson

The phone call came at 10:30 on a Wednesday morning. "It's the baby," Scott said flatly. "Something's wrong. I'm on my way to the emergency room. Meet me there."

Laura sat at her desk and stared, the telephone cradled limply in her hand. *What could it be?* Timothy had been fine that morning. Her mind raced as she jumped in the car for the 20-minute drive to the hospital.

When Timothy was six weeks old, Laura returned to her job as an administrative assistant at the community college. That was six weeks ago; Timothy was three months old and doing well with the sitter. *She should have put him down for a nap by now,* Laura thought. *What could have happened?*

Anguished thoughts swirled in her mind. *I shouldn't have left him with a sitter,* she thought accusingly. *Whatever happened, it's my fault.*

Scott and Laura were both 26. They had met in college and married just after graduation. They came to the Lord together during premarital counseling and were involved in a good church. Scott's career as an electrical engineer was going well. Timothy was healthy. Now what?

An emergency room nurse met her at the door with a somber expression.

"Where's my baby?" Laura said, emotion rising in her voice. "I want to see my baby!"

As the doors of the examining room swung open, one look told Laura the truth. Scott's helpless appearance. The doctor's pained expression. And Timothy — so still.

"We've done everything we can," the wearied doctor said. "I'm sorry. Timothy's gone."

Laura moved slowly toward the gurney where Timothy lay. She looked down at the lifeless body of her three-month-old son.

Picking him up gently, she held him to her chest. Scott moved from the other side of the gurney and wrapped his arms around his wife and son.

"No," Laura sobbed, gently rocking the tiny body. "No." She said it again. "He's not gone. I'm not ready to let him go."

THE EFFECT OF LOSS

Scott and Laura learned that their son died of SIDS — Sudden Infant Death Syndrome. In an instant their world changed. The child they planned for and birthed and cared for was gone, and their hopes for the future were gone with him. From that day forward, their lives would be defined by this sad point of reference.

Nothing can prepare the human heart for the loss of a loved one. Even if the death has been expected for a long time, the moment of its arrival is always sudden. Just like that, life ends — sometimes just as it's beginning.

Death steals from us not only the present but also the future. The child who held such promise is taken. The daughter who would be given away at the altar will never grow up. The mother who gave stability and comfort is gone. The father who provided advice, discipline, and income is never coming home.

Those who are left to pick up the pieces soon realize that the funeral isn't the end of the pain. This wound is not easily healed.

Each person's grief is unique. No two of us experience loss in just the same way. Yet grief brings with it some predictable emotions. Nearly every person who experiences loss will suffer some of these side effects.

Denial

Scott and Laura's immediate reaction to the loss of their son was *No!* That is a common response to death. As they held their child and each other, it was as if they were saying, *We refuse to acknowledge that he's gone. We refuse to begin living as if our lives have changed. We are not ready to make the painful decisions that have to be made.*

Questioning

Scott and Laura had always relied on their faith. Now questions crept in. We question God — *Why? Why did this happen?* We question others — *Where were you? Why didn't you help?* We question life — *What's the point?* We question ourselves — *Can I handle this?*

Anger

At some point, these questions are likely to take on an accusing tone. We spar with God over His responsibility. *How could You do this? Why did You let this happen? Where were You when I needed You? What kind of God are You?*

God is not the only target. Survivors may harbor resentment against anyone they contrive to be responsible as well as imagined enemies. *How dare they act as if nothing is wrong? He never loved Dad, and I'll never forgive him.*

Jealousy

Jealousy makes its appearance in everyday places — maybe the mall, a restaurant, or in church. A child is helped into a booster seat at the restaurant, and you wonder, *Why do they get to have a healthy baby?* A middle-aged woman sits in a coffee shop with her daughter, and you think, *It's not fair that my mother is gone.* The bitter seed of jealousy produces a weed that poisons relationships and strangles the heart with isolation.

Depression

"After about a week," Laura recalls, "I shut the door to Timothy's room. I just shut the door and refused to go in." At first, Laura didn't even know that she was depressed. It came over her gradually. First, it became easier to watch the evening news than to converse at the dinner table. Then it was more convenient to lunch by herself than to be with friends. Eventually, going to work became almost unbearable. Finally, she slept all she could as an antidote to pain.

More than just a case of the blues, depression brings its own set of symptoms: apathy, despair, fatigue, lethargy, withdrawal.

Guilt

Another emotion blindsided Laura. She began to feel guilt — misplaced though it was — about leaving her child with a baby-sitter. The guilt threatened to suffocate her. *You should have been there. You deserted your child. He needed you; now he's gone.* Irrational though they were, the feelings of guilt were very real.

Guilt, false or real, produces shame. Shame produces withdrawal. We withdraw from others. We withdraw into ourselves. We withdraw into substance abuse. We try to hide our feelings of neglect or shame behind someone or something.

GOD'S WORD

Laura was not the first woman to lose a son.

Since Eden, the experience of loss is one of the constants of human existence.

No passage of Scripture deals more pointedly with the experience of loss than the story of two sisters, Mary and Martha; their brother, Lazarus; and the faithful friend who seemed strangely absent during their time of need — Jesus.

After the death of Lazarus, Mary and Martha experienced emotions familiar to those of everyone who has suffered the loss of a loved one. Yet they arrived at point of healing, the place where recovery begins. For them, that point was called hope. Their story is recorded in John 11:1−27. It reveals valuable lessons for dealing with our own pain.

Death Is Not a Personal Punishment

Lazarus was one of Jesus' closest friends. They had lunched together in the marketplace, no doubt, and swapped funny stories. Jesus had been a guest in his home. When the sisters sent word to Jesus that Lazarus was sick, they described him as "the one you love" (John 11:3). Jesus had a special relationship with this family. In fact, Lazarus' sister Mary was the same one who had poured perfume on Jesus' feet and wiped them with her hair (v. 2; see Luke 7:38).

She had much for which to be forgiven, and Jesus forgave it all.

But their close proximity to Jesus did not prevent the pain of loss. Although Jesus loved Lazarus and his sisters, Lazarus was gone. Clearly, Lazarus's death was not an evidence of God's judgment on their home.

One of the first tricks that Satan plays on a grieving mind is the suggestion that death is a form of personal punishment. "Your mother died because you were a lousy son." "This is what you get for sowing your wild oats." "If you had prayed more, this wouldn't have happened."

The account of Lazarus makes it very clear that death is not meted out as a personal punishment. It *is* true that death is the result of human sin (see Gen. 3). But that's a judgment that affects all people equally — whether or not they're believers. All people must die a physical death regardless of how righteously they lived (Heb. 9:27). In His mercy, the Heavenly Father graciously heals some people, miraculously delaying the moment of death. Yet all will die, even His most beloved children.

Are you grieving right now? Know this: your loved one did not die because God singled you or your loved one out for punishment. We die because of sin and the

misery that it has inflicted on the world —
a misery for which there is an ultimate
remedy.

God Is Not As Far Away as He Seems

Death, terrible as it seems to us, is merely
one thread in the fabric of time and eternity.
God does not fear death. In His mind, there
are some things even worse than death —
unbelief, for example.

So when Jesus heard that His friend Lazarus was ill, He waited for two days to go to
Bethany, even though it was only two miles
away. When Jesus finally arrived in Bethany,
Martha ran to meet Him. Without a greet-
ing, she blurted out the words that are both
an accusation and an affirmation of hope:
"Lord, if you had been here, my brother
would not have died."

Even in despair, Martha could not quite
let go of hope. The Creator who grew
beauty from barrenness could create something purposeful even from something that
was so pitiful and painful.

Like Martha, we often blame God for
what He didn't do even as we hope that He
may do something yet. That emotion is
reflected often in bedside prayers and even
in funeral prayers. We wonder where God
is, yet we continue to hope that He'll arrive,

even at a late hour, and provide healing or comfort.

Yet the awkward two-day interval was not a demonstration of Jesus' inaction. He already had a plan in mind, as He told His disciples before they left for Bethany: "It is for God's glory so that God's Son may be glorified through it" (John 11:4). Christ was already brooding over the troubled waters of Mary and Martha's lives. He knew He was going to make a mercy move and create something good from the emptiness of their loss.

God sometimes allows our circumstances to unravel beyond the point where we can cope with them, because otherwise we would solve our own problems and perhaps not turn to God or give Him glory. Yet when we suffer, we know that we need God. This is the point where His glory may be revealed.

Before Lazarus died, Jesus had already planned to comfort the sisters. He knew that He would bring Lazarus back to life. Would Mary and Martha hold on long enough to enjoy the saving spectacle?

Although He may seem far away right now, God is already at work in your life. He will take steps to bring you comfort, and He has provided the gift of eternal life

70

through Christ's death and resurrection. Can you hold on long enough to see God at work?

Jesus Will Provide What You Need

Withdrawal, guilt, anger, questions. Both sisters felt these emotions after Lazarus died. But they reacted to them differently. When the news came that Jesus had arrived, Mary stayed at home — brooding, perhaps, and sorrowful. Martha, always the doer (see Luke 10:38–42), ran to meet Jesus, ready to vent her anger.

Jesus met both sisters at their point of need. To Martha's questions, Jesus provided answers. He challenged her mind to believe in possibilities she had never considered. He met her on the path of intellectual conflict.

Later Mary summoned the courage to venture from the cocoon of her home. This wasn't the first time that she had met Jesus. She knew His track record! She had poured both her tears and her gratitude at His feet. He had restored her, forgiven her, and made her whole. She repeated the gesture now, hurling herself at His feet, weeping. When He saw the depth of her sorrow, Jesus was deeply moved in spirit and troubled. In response, He performed His greatest

miracle. Jesus met Mary on her path also —
the path of overwhelming sorrow. To both
women He provided the comfort they
needed.

Loss isn't a time to stay at home. It's a
time to hit the road — to make your way to
the Savior's side. Wherever you are on the
journey to healing, Jesus will meet you. He
will provide comfort for your broken spirit.
He will provide the strength and resources
you need to face the future. Yet, like Martha
and Mary, you must take a step toward
Him. Will you reach out to Jesus in hope?
Will you trust Him for your future?

Trusting God

Both Mary and Martha made the same
statement upon meeting Jesus: "Lord, if you
had been here, my brother would not have
died" (vv. 21, 32). Jesus responded to Martha's statement with a bold assertion of His
own: "Your brother will rise again" (v. 23).

Martha was a believer in God. She knew
about life after death, and she thought Jesus
was talking about heaven. But Jesus' next
statement ignited the spark of faith. "I am
the resurrection and the life. He who believes in me will live, even though he dies;
and whoever lives and believes in me will
never die" (vv. 25–26). Lazarus' death was

not the end — it was the beginning. God would have the last word in this loss!

As the hope slowly dawned on Mary, Jesus asked the question that each of us must someday answer: "Do you believe this?" (v. 26).

The question was no longer general; it was personal. It was no longer a vague belief in some distant future. The question was about right here, right now. Did she believe that Jesus Christ has power over life and death?

Do you?

When you're faced with a personal loss, all your questions will be personal and immediate. The childhood notion about "a place in the sky" will not sustain you when faced with the death of a spouse, a child, a parent, a brother. You'll need a personal faith in the personal God who has the power to enter your life at any point and perform a miracle.

Mary and Martha witnessed the miracle of resurrection. Jesus went on to issue that glorious command that brought life back from death — "Lazarus, come forth!" You have not had that privilege, but you can still have that faith. God has power to control death and life. Death is not the end for a believer in Christ; it's the beginning of a new life.

You may be facing a loss so great that it seems final — eternal. Yet there is hope. God has promised that by faith we will live again.

Do you believe that? Will you dare to believe that the future can be better than the present? Will you trust God? Will you hold on to hope?

STEPS TO HEALING

Few of us have dramatic stories to tell about our meetings with God. Yet many who grieve can report experiences not unlike Mary and Martha's, times when God met them on the path to healing. These stories typically include some common elements; these steps toward healing have been trodden by many lonely mourners. You may find them to be good first steps on your road to recovery from loss.

Maintain an Attitude of Faith

Loss brings overwhelming sorrow, and that will almost certainly prompt doubts about God — His goodness and His faithfulness. But a loss in your life doesn't have to bring a loss of *faith*. Even the disciples doubted at times (see Matt. 28:17). Believers who have experienced loss speak often of the difference between grieving in despair and griev-

ing in hope. The first is a denial of faith —
"I think there's no use in trusting God."
The second is an affirmation of faith —
"Lord, I don't know where You are or what
You're doing, but I know You'll show up
soon!"

The apostle Paul made that distinction to
some of the early Christians who were
troubled by questions about death. He
wrote, "Brothers, we do not want you to be
ignorant about those who fall asleep, or to
grieve like the rest of men, who have no
hope. We believe that Jesus died and rose
again and so we believe that God will bring
with Jesus those who have fallen asleep in
him" (1 Thess. 4:13–14).

In your grief, and even in your doubt,
continue to reach out to God. Trust Him,
even though He seems far away. He'll be
there soon.

Accept the Comfort of Others

Sadly, the grief of loss may be compounded
by marital conflict. An alarming number of
couples who lose a child later divorce. Loss
is difficult to bear in any circumstance.
Satan always attacks our weakest point. For
many husbands and wives, that weak link is
the bond between them.

Others are driven by grief to withdraw

from a community of family and friends. Depression causes them to isolate themselves when what they need most is the support of caring friends.

Solitude is a valuable tool for recovery, but it can become a lonely trap. Although it may be difficult at first, accept the support of others. Pray with them, and ask them to pray for you. Talk about your grief with your spouse or other family members. Take advantage of the marvelous, free support group called church. Let others help you on your road to healing.

Seek the Wisdom of Scripture

Laura especially recalls the advice of one friend. "I was listening carefully to the first thing she said to me, because I knew I could trust her advice."

That proved to be true. Laura's lifelong friend, Janet, sent her a card with a specially chosen verse:

In this you greatly rejoice, though now for a little while you may have had to suffer grief in all kinds of trials. These have come so that your faith — of greater worth than gold, which perishes even though refined by fire — may be proved genuine and may result in praise, glory and honor

76

when Jesus Christ is revealed *(1 Pet. 1:6–7).*

"That has become my life verse," Laura said. "That's what helped me begin to look to the future."

Scripture gives many promises to those who grieve. Read from the Psalms, the Gospel of John, 1 and 2 Thessalonians, Philippians, and other comforting scriptures. God's Word is powerful and effective. It will empower you to hope.

Cherish the Past, but Look to the Future

Before leaving the emergency room, Laura took a lock of Timothy's hair. It's one of her treasured possessions. It may help to develop some rituals that honor the memory of the one you lost. Photographs can be especially important mementos of a lost loved one.

At the same time, look to the future. Don't allow the past to become your hope — it never will be. Learn to cherish the past without worshiping it. Love what was lost, but let it go.

Accept the Unanswered Questions

There's no good reason for the death of a child or anyone else, so don't invent one.

Rom. 8:28 tells us that in all things God works for good for those who love Him and are called according to His purpose. It is our promise of God's loving control over every aspect of our lives, but it is not a facile response to unanswerable questions. Why did Timothy die? Why did your mother die? What good will come from the tragic death of your brother? Ultimately, we must patiently accept the questions for which there are no answers this side of heaven. As Laura said, "You may not know the reason until you get to heaven, and then you probably won't need to know." For now, simply believe that God is always good. He is.

Give Thanks for Growth

"I'm an expert on losing a child to SIDS," Laura Johnson says calmly. "It wasn't my choice; I never wanted this, of course. But it gives me an opportunity to help others."

Your experience has probably made you an expert in some area of loss. You may have gained knowledge about caring for a terminally ill loved one. Perhaps you've been forced to grow by accepting greater responsibility after the death of a parent. Even in your suffering, you have changed for the better. Thank God for it.

And help others if you can. Paul wrote,

"Praise be to the God and Father of our Lord Jesus Christ, the Father of compassion and the God of all comfort, who comforts us in all our troubles, so that we can comfort those in any trouble with the comfort we ourselves have received from God" (2 Cor. 1:3–4). Perhaps the experience you have gained at such great cost can be used to lessen the pain of another.

Give It Time

Your grief will never be completely over in the sense that you will never again feel the sting of pain. The memory of loss will always bring sorrow. But it will lessen over time.

If you want a benchmark for "feeling better," don't use one year. That's not enough time to process the absence of a person from birthdays, holidays, and family gatherings. Two years is a more realistic time frame for beginning to feel "normal."

Laura recalls, "A few years after Timothy's death, I was with a woman who had just lost a child. She was a mess." Without being judgmental, Laura says, "When I saw how broken she was and how hurt, I thought, *Wow — I've really come a long way.*"

Your grief won't go away. It will hurt less and hurt less often. But there's no way to completely remove the pain of losing a human being. Grief over human suffering and death is what drove our own Savior to the Cross.

THE POINT OF HEALING

Every Sunday for six months, Scott and Laura drove to the cemetery after church. They looked at the grave and tended the flowers. "We were parents," Laura explained, "and that's what parents do — they look after their children." In one sense, the ritual was a form of therapy for them. They used the time to remember their child, they shed plenty of tears, and the weekly visits brought the two of them closer.

At another level, the cemetery visits were a symbol of their growing attachment to the past. "I'll never forget the first Sunday we didn't go," Laura recalls. "I had become pregnant again, and I was very tired. It was a rainy day, so we decided to go straight home after church. I felt guilty all afternoon." Without realizing it, Laura was becoming trapped in her devotion to Timothy. Her focus on the past was preventing her from living in the present and looking to the future.

As we often do, Laura had looked for a physical remedy to her spiritual need.

Believing that having another child would ease the pain of losing Timothy, she and Scott determined to have another child as soon as possible. Six months after Timothy's death, she was three months pregnant but no less miserable. "I thought having another baby would solve everything," Laura explains. "It didn't. Even though I was carrying another child, all I could see was Timothy's face." Unable to look forward to a new life, she could only grieve for the one that was lost.

"I knew that wasn't good," Laura confessed, "but it's all I could do."

There is a point of healing for loss. And that is hope. Laura reached that point of healing in an unusual place — a bookstore.

Scott and Laura had already picked out names for the new baby. If it was a girl, they would name her Amanda. Still curious about the name, Laura picked up a baby name book while browsing a bookstore. She looked up the name and read the meaning. There, hemmed in by the crowded shelves, away from the uncomfortable looks of her friends, God spoke Laura's name.

It wasn't called aloud, but she heard it just the same. It was as if He had passed a note to her across the table in the school library and whispered, *Here, Laura — read this.* The words on the page read, "Amanda: worthy of love." What Laura heard was the voice of God saying, *Laura, Timothy is with Me. He's fine. Don't worry about him. The child I have given you is worthy of your love. She needs your attention now.*

And the healing came. The pain began to seep away, replaced by a refreshing current of hope. Six months later, Amanda Christine was born — the child who was worthy of love. The name that the Lord gave her became a symbol of hope. Laura began to look to the future.

"There in the bookstore, I finally accepted the truth that I'll see Timothy again. I can give him to God because I know that death is not the end." It was a beautiful benediction of peace for Laura and Scott. They had reached the point of healing for those who experience loss. They had reached the point of hope.

Sixteen years have passed since Timothy's death, and God has blessed Scott and Laura with two more children. Their marriage is stronger than ever. They'll tell you that life is good.

They still miss Timothy, but their memories are colored by hope, not pain. "When I feel like talking about Timothy, I wear this," she says, pointing to a mother's pin with three birthstones. "Every time I wear this pin, someone will ask how many children I have. 'Three,' I tell them. 'And one is a perfect angel.' "

Her contented smile is a picture of grace. God gave her three children. One was taken away. Now she lives with the hope of seeing him again in heaven.

That's a picture of the good life for those who grieve. It is not a denial of death or an absence of pain, but a life marked more by joy than by sorrow, a life lived with hope.

That life may seem unimaginable to you now, locked in a dungeon of despair. But you *will* get there. Hold on to hope, reach out to others, trust God to do the right thing, and your heart will heal. Jesus will meet you on your path to healing.

Your Journey

Exploring Your Story

1. How is your story of loss similar to Scott and Laura Johnson's? How is it different?

2. What emotions have you felt after the death of a loved one? Which were the strongest?

3. How has losing a loved one affected your relationships with others? With God?

Exploring God's Word

1. Read John 11:1–45. Why do you think Jesus delayed going to Bethany after He heard that Lazarus was sick?

2. How would you describe Mary's reaction to Jesus' arrival? How would you describe Martha's?

3. What did Jesus mean by saying, "I am the resurrection and the life"? (v. 25).

Exploring the Steps to Healing

1. Of the action steps listed in this chapter, which ones seem the best to you? Which ones seem the hardest? Why?

2. Have you made the decision to hold on to hope? If so, describe when that thought formed in your mind. If not, why not?

3. What is the first thing you must do to begin the process of healing in your heart? When will you do it?

4
REJECTION
FROM BITTERNESS TO ACCEPTANCE

Point of Healing
I refuse to believe that nobody loves me
because I know that God does.

I felt that this bitterness was mine; it was
something I had to keep. Then it dawned
on me that I could just let it go.
— Janet Forsythe

"When you first came to live with us, I
hated you. I never wanted you here. But I
have to admit that you've become quite a
nice young lady."

Janet Forsythe seethed with anger. *Was
that supposed to be a compliment?* Janet had
imagined that the evening of her senior
prom would be different. That on this, of all
nights, her foster mother might show some
affection, might treat her as one of the family. As she sat in her bedroom, wearing a

85

borrowed dress and shoes, the pretty 18-year-old stared blankly at the woman she had called Mom for 10 years. Behind a mask of practiced indifference, memories of rejection surfaced.

She recalled the incident at a McDonald's restaurant where her "new mommy" had taken her years before. What she had hoped would be a celebration of her new family became the first reminder of her real place in the world. "It was Ralph's idea," she overheard her foster mother say to a friend. "I didn't want her."

Janet remembered the years of harsh treatment by this emotionally distant woman. Desperate for love and affection, Janet tried hard to be good, to do things right, to be lovable. Instead, she was treated as a guest or intruder, isolated emotionally, berated constantly, spanked for every minor misbehavior. She remembered 10 Christmases of watching "the real children" open lavish presents while she received token gifts. She remembered sitting alone while her foster brothers were smothered with hugs and kisses. She remembered the constant fear that her foster mother would erupt in anger, belittling her with words while Janet's ineffectual foster father pretended to be occupied. *I lived in fear of you,* she thought, *but no more.*

Other memories crept into Janet's mind. She vaguely remembered her own mother, whose manic-depressive disorder had forced Janet into the Oregon Children's Institution at age two. She thought of the curious mix of love and anger for this woman who would not — could not — provide a home for her child. She remembered other children at the orphanage, some of whom found adoptive parents. She recalled the pain of abandonment and asking herself as she fell asleep, *Why doesn't anybody love me?*

And she remembered "him" — the big, handsome man who had visited her at the children's home. She remembered his pretty wife and her pretty dress and the trips to the park. She remembered that she rode on his shoulders and played games and ate ice cream. And they came back the next week. And back again. "Are you going to adopt me?" Janet asked childishly. That was their last visit. The handsome man never came back again.

Tears slid into the corners of Janet's eyes. She blinked them away, still staring vacantly at the woman who pretended to be her mother. *I hate you,* she screamed inside. *I hate you for mistreating me, I hate you for not loving me, and I hate you most of all for pretending now that you do.*

A car door slammed in the driveway. "I'm leaving now" was all she said.

THE EFFECT OF REJECTION

Rejection comes in various packages. The divorce decree arrives in the mail. The manager calls you to her office to give you your walking papers.

Sometimes rejection is seen in the absence of something or someone: no present under the tree, no card arriving in the mail, an empty chair at the table, a phone that won't ring. Constant reminders of a punishing reality — the one you love does not love you. Have you felt the sting of rejection by a parent, a lover, a friend, a brother or sister, a spouse, even an employer?

Rejection shrivels the spirit. Once the shock of denial subsides, bitter feelings begin to grow in the heart. This wound leaves lasting scars. Here are a few of the marks of rejection.

Resentment

Janet's resentment spread over her like the web of a spider. Self-pity became her companion. From that fertile ground, anger grew. Finally the web was complete — she hated her foster mother for what she had done to her.

"I knew there was nothing wrong with me," Janet says, reflecting on her relationship with her foster mother. "I knew I was lovable. I was angry at her for not loving me."

Janet is not alone. Family photos have captured many a fake smile. Brother, sister, spouse, or parent is only an arm's length away, but the emotional distance may be immeasurable.

Bitterness

Bitterness is another fruit of rejection. Bitterness is a healthy dose of frustration mixed with envy. Having been rejected, we view even those with no connection to us as competitors in the game of life. It seems so unfair that they should enjoy the affirmation and affection we've been denied.

For Janet, even a happy marriage and two healthy daughters didn't lessen the suffering from her old wounds. "When I realized how good my family life was, it made the pain worse in some ways," Janet recalls. "When I looked at my own children, resentment and bitter thoughts reared their heads — *Why wouldn't anybody love me the way I love them?*"

For the bitter person, a look in the mirror begs the anguished question *What's wrong with me? Why won't anybody love me?*

Low Self-esteem

We humans characteristically see ourselves through the eyes of others. When others approve of us, we feel good. When others reject us, we conclude that they must see in us something that we can't. *They don't think I'm worth very much. Maybe they're right.*

The mirror becomes a mortal enemy as the battle of worth is waged each day. We fight the war with an arsenal of personal care products. New makeup. A different hairstyle. Expensive clothes. *I'll make myself more lovable. Then someone will want me.*

Perfectionism

There must be something wrong with me is a typical reaction to rejection. We assume that we've neglected something. We feel that we've failed somehow, and someone else has seconded the motion. A common response is to try to be perfect. "I tried to do everything right," Janet says. "I was afraid that if I did something wrong or offended anyone, they wouldn't love me." Thousands of people live by that misguided strategy. They become oversensitive: *Did I say something* wrong? They overachieve: *It's no bother, really.* They're self-critical: *I'm sorry — it's all my fault.* They live in bondage to others: *Is everything OK? You're not mad, are you?*

Everyone we meet is a critic as we strive to meet their demands, real or imagined. We live for the approval that always seems to be withheld.

Fear

Attractive and popular though she was, Janet Forsythe refused to believe that anyone could truly love her. When she met Jack Fletcher in college, she first ignored and then avoided his attention. "He had to propose to me three times before I would believe that he meant it," she recalls.

Rejection not only affects the soul but affects social ability as well. It has an underlying influence on our relationships. For example, it becomes easier to avoid relationships than to risk failure. We don't ask for a date because we fear rejection. We don't apply for a better job because we're afraid of being turned down. We avoid close friendships because that would make us vulnerable. We're afraid to make emotional commitments because we may be betrayed.

Embarrassment

"I always felt different," Janet says. "I just wanted to be normal, like everybody else." The person who has suffered rejection is always wary of the glances of others, always feels himself or herself to be the subject of whispered conversations. *Everybody knows. I can't go anywhere. I'm tired of being pitied.*

Regardless of who is at fault in a broken relationship, the rejected person believes that others will blame him or her. The unemployed man feels embarrassed. *I don't want people to know I got fired.* "A man takes pride in his work" is more than an axiom; it's a fact of life. The duty of employment weighs heavily upon the husband or father — winding all the way back to the Garden of Eden and God's edict to the first man: "By the sweat of your brow you will eat your food" (Gen. 3:19). The loss of a job, even for the most benign reasons, brings feelings of rejection, humiliation.

Loneliness

Rejection, finally, leaves one alone. The attention, companionship, camaraderie, or love that was sought is withheld. Loneliness is the result. The apostle Paul once found himself deserted by a trusted friend. He wrote to his aide, Timothy, "Do your best to come to me quickly, for Demas, because he loved this world, has deserted me and has gone to Thessalonica. Crescens has gone to Galatia, and Titus to Dalmatia" (2 Tim. 4:9–10). The names and places are different, but the feeling of loneliness is just the same today. Rejected. Deserted. Friendless. Janet Forsythe's question echoes in many hearts: *Why won't somebody love me?*

GOD'S WORD

As long as there have been human relationships, there's been rejection. The Bible records dozens of cases. Joseph was rejected by his brothers. Leah was rejected by her husband, Jacob. Even Jesus was rejected by His own people. One of the most painful stories of rejection is the story of Hagar, the servant of Sarai (later called Sarah). This story has all the makings of a tragic drama: a young girl living far from home, a wealthy household, a bitter mistress, infidelity, treachery, disloyalty. And there's one more element: grace. Hagar's story is found in Gen. 16 and offers a solid rock of hope for those who have been rejected: God loves you, even when others don't.

Everyone Suffers Rejection
Abram (later called Abraham) and Sarai

(later known as Sarah) were good people. They were God's people. God called Abram to be the father of a great nation, to inherit the Promised Land. But like all real people, they were flawed.

God had promised that Abram and Sarai would have a son, but the years were slipping by quickly. Sarai was advancing in age and still hadn't conceived a child. Their ill-thought plan was to hurry God's promise of a son by allowing Abram to sleep with Hagar, the young girl who tended Sarai. Hagar would bear the child, but Sarai would raise the child as her own. An accepted practice in those days, this ancient form of family engineering would have disastrous consequences.

At first, Hagar was an obedient servant responding to the orders of her mistress. But the circumstances changed quickly, and Hagar was partly to blame. She added insult to the injury of the situation by lording her pregnancy over the barren Sarai. Sarai's resentment was born in the humiliation she felt for being without children. Soon Sarai's anger gave way to abuse, and Hagar's faithfulness turned to fear. When the situation became intolerable, Hagar fled.

Rejection is a fact of life. For better or for worse, most of us will face it at some time.

It is often undeserved and unexpected. Mark Sheldon was a youth counselor whose reputation was rock solid. He never second-guessed his supervisor; he always did what was expected of him. When his boss asked him to spend some time with Jeremy, a young man who was addicted to cocaine, Mark readily agreed. He knew that he would have to make himself vulnerable in order to minister to Jeremy, but he was determined to carry out his assignment.

When he wasn't high, Jeremy was a warm, outgoing, and caring kid. It was a different story when he was under the influence of cocaine. Week after week, Mark struggled to cope with Jeremy's mood swings, his manic depression, even going to the emergency room when Jeremy overdosed.

"Mark, could I see you?" The supervisor called the teen counselor into his office one morning. "There's something I need to discuss with you."

Mark was unprepared for the news he would receive. "Jeremy was arrested for possession of cocaine last night. He told the police that he bought it from you."

Mark was stunned.

"I don't believe him," the supervisor continued, "but my hands are tied. I'll have to suspend you until we complete the investigation."

It was a double blow. Mark felt as if his boss didn't believe in him, and he knew that Jeremy had betrayed his trust. Being a good counselor, a good employee, and even a faithful friend had not ensured that Mark would never be disbelieved, disliked, or rejected.

It can happen to anyone. Rejection by a human being is not an indication of your worth in God's eyes. Hagar was rejected by Sarai — but she was loved by God.

God Will Always Love You

Hagar — miserable, tired, and resentful — ran away into the desert. Tired from her journey, burdened by the consequence of her actions, and fearful for the future of her unborn child, Hagar found her way to a wayside spring. But she needed more than the refreshment of water for her tired body. She needed relief for her anguished soul. She needed to know that her life had value — that she was needed, that she was wanted, that she was loved. She needed a God-sized love to soothe the ache she felt.

There at the spring the angel of the Lord sat down beside Hagar. This "angel of the LORD," who appears mysteriously in several scriptures (see Gen. 22:11; Exod. 3:2; 2 Sam. 24:16) was probably the preincarnate Christ. He knew all about Hagar and her condition. He knew that she was expecting a child. What's more, He knew all about the boy who would be born to her. "You shall name him Ishmael," he said, "for the LORD has heard of your misery" (Gen. 16:11).

"You are the God who sees me," Hagar said (v. 13).

She had fled to the desert feeling miserable and alone. But she wasn't alone. God was there. He looked. He saw her. He listened to the cry of her heart. And He came to her.

What a thought! God sees you. He knows you. He understands where you are, what has happened in your life, and even what will happen next. What assurance! When you feel lonely, alone, deserted by friends, family, a lover — God sees. When you cry at night, asking that pitiful question *Why doesn't anybody love me?* God hears. His arms are bigger than your problems. His ears hear your tiniest whispers. You have a standing appointment at the Great Physician's office. God knows you. God loves you. When it seems that no other person cares, God does.

You Must Try Again

Charles Haddon Spurgeon once quipped, "By perseverance, the snail reached the Ark." It's by persevering that we come into some of the better things God has to offer. Hagar, meeting God in the desert, received comfort — but not a free ride. God had a job for her to do. "Go back to your mistress and submit to her," the angel told Hagar (v. 9). Those couldn't have been welcome words for Hagar, guest of honor at her own pity party.

But there was more. The angel added, "I will so increase your descendants that they will be too numerous to count" (v. 10). God showed compassion, but it was followed with a commission. He called her to blossom in the desert, to grow even in the place of her gloom. He calls us as well. Even at the point of our greatest rejection, He gives us a cause. We're called to persevere, not pout.

Invariably, God responds to our cries for help with two things: the comfort of His presence and the command to move on. Hagar was given both, and so are you.

Steps to Healing

Hagar would never overcome the bitterness of her broken relationship with Abram and

98

Sarai by running away. To find peace, she had to get up from the roadside rest stop, make a U-turn, and go back to face the problem.

If you're to find healing for your broken heart, you'll need to take some action too. Mark Twain said, "Twenty years from now you will be more disappointed by the things that you didn't do than by the ones you did do. So throw off the bowlines. Sail away from the safe harbor. Catch the trade winds in your sails. Explore. Dream. Discover." Here are some steps to begin that journey to wholeness.

Don't Give in to Self-pity

"Nobody loves me" is the lament of the rejected one. The cry is more of self-pity than reality. Self-pity is a perfectly natural emotion, but a crippling one. Like a narcotic, self-pitying thoughts are comforting at first, addictive in the end. It's tempting to wallow, like Hagar, in self-centered thought that life revolves around you and your misfortunes.

It's never true that no one loves you, because God always does. The apostle Paul reminds us, "Who shall separate us from the love of Christ? Shall trouble or hardship or persecution or famine or nakedness or danger or sword? As it is written: 'For your sake we face death all day long; we are considered as sheep to be slaughtered.' No, in all these things we are more than conquerors through him who loved us" (Rom. 8:35–37).

Because you've been rejected by a friend, employer, lover, or family member does not mean that you're friendless, useless, unlovely, and alone. Don't waste precious time on the luxury of feeling sorry for yourself.

Believe in Yourself

"There are two directions you can go after being rejected," Janet reflects. "One is to hold on to it and to try to cope with it, looking for love in the wrong places — drugs, relationships, with men. I always knew that I was going to do something better."

Low self-esteem is a plague for those who have been rejected. Desperate to find self-worth, they look for it in the worst places — casual sex, abusive relationships, and substance abuse. Believe in yourself. Know that your life has worth and purpose. Don't accept the image of yourself as one who is unlovely or unlovable. Don't allow other people to define your life for you. Choose to be an achiever, a winner, not a whiner.

Nick Barton was a youth sponsor at a

church in Ottawa, Ontario. On a Saturday evening he opened his door and greeted one of the college students in his young adult group. "Eddie! I didn't expect you to come home this weekend!"

"I guess my folks didn't expect me either," the boy replied softly. "They're gone."

"What do you mean?" Nick asked.

Eddie sat on the front porch chair, his head bowed, "They moved," he said tearfully. "My parents moved out of our house — and they didn't even tell me. I have no idea where they are."

"You're kidding, right?" Nick quizzed. But he wasn't kidding. Eddie's stepfather had disliked the boy for years. While Eddie was away at school, the family had moved out of their rented quarters. Eddie came home from college to an empty house.

"He always said he would get rid of me, one way or another. I guess he did."

Eddie could have left his life there on the porch. He didn't. The youth sponsor gave him a temporary room. Eddie went back to school after the Easter break and graduated the next spring — with honors. "It hurt," Eddie admits. "It hurt a lot. But I knew I had to keep going. I didn't want that moment to define my whole life."

101

Winning was more important than whining.

Let Go of Bitterness

If you choose to hold on to bitterness, you must understand the dangers. It will poison your spirit and spread to every part of you. Or you can let it go. Resentment is not a tattoo on your spirit. You can peel it off if you choose. Make the decision to look forward instead of back.

"It took me 10 years to let go of the anger," Gordon Bryce admits. "That's how long I stewed over being dropped by my first girlfriend." Gordon was 19 years old and looking forward to going home on his first break from college. On Friday night he called Ellen, his girlfriend, who still lived at home. "I don't think we should see each other when you get back," she said slowly. "In fact, I don't think this relationship is going to work out."

"I was humiliated," Gordon said. "For years, I carried the pain of that rejection. It sounds foolish now, but I hated Ellen for what she did to me. Every time I heard her name, my stomach knotted up." Ten years later, Gordon had a moment that changed his life. "I realized that my anger wasn't hurting Ellen — it was hurting me. I was the one with the anxiety. I was suffering for my anger, not her."

Bitterness does nothing to make it right, even the score, or get back at the one who hurt you. It harms only you. Let it go.

Try Again

"My husband loved me from day one," Janet says. Surprisingly, that's a gift many people have trouble accepting. That was true of Janet, who at first rejected her husband's affection. "I didn't think anyone would love me," she explains.

It's a common reaction. When someone you've sought has rejected your attention, will anyone else accept it?

- If I'm not good enough for this job, am I good enough for anything?

- If she doesn't love me, what would any woman see in me?

- It hurts too much to try again.

Seeking relationships of any kind is risky. Submitting a job application, asking for a date, and inviting someone to your home have this in common: they each carry the risk of rejection. You put your heart on the line every time you offer yourself to another person.

Fear of failure keeps us paralyzed in a state of rejection. If you will experience love and acceptance, you must risk being rejected again. No one can love you if you won't let them. You must take the risk of allowing others into your life. You must attempt new relationships, new experiences, new jobs — even a new love.

Try.

THE POINT OF HEALING

For years Janet's relationship with her foster mother continued sporadically. Their occasional meetings left Janet paralyzed with anxiety. "I prayed to forgive her," Janet confesses, "but in my heart I knew I never had."

Then one Sunday Janet's pastor preached about forgiveness. When he gave an invitation, Janet was the first to respond. She recalls the emotions she felt that day. "For years I thought I had to cope with this awful bitterness that I lived with. Suddenly it dawned on me — I don't have to cope with it; I can just let it go. I prayed, *Lord, I know You don't want me to carry this resentment. I don't want it either, so I'm giving it up to You.*

From that point on, life became a joy to Janet. Her children grew. Her marriage blossomed. Life was good. But sometimes God can't leave well enough alone. He not only gave Janet a new future but also a new past to go with it.

Eight years after Janet was released from bitterness, she told her story to some friends at church. The details sounded familiar to Chuck Weld, but he refused to believe it could be true. Thirty years earlier, Chuck and Rhonda Weld had been a childless couple hoping to adopt. They had even visited a little girl several times at the Oregon Children's Institution. Then Rhonda was stricken with cancer. Within a year, Chuck lost both his wife and the beautiful child he had come to think of as "my little girl." Chuck married again and fathered four children, divorced, and married for the third time, to Phyllis. Now he was faced with the nagging question — *could Janet Forsythe be the child I've loved for all these years?*

"Go to the children's home and find out," Phyllis insisted. "You lost her once — don't lose her again."

The news took Janet's breath away. Not only was "the man" still alive, but he was living in the same town with her, *attending the same church!* And there was more — he still wanted her to be his little girl.

"Of course I want you to adopt me!" Janet shrieked. Not even the judge could believe the story when she signed a brand-new certificate to record the birth of Janet Weld.

"I've respected Chuck Weld for all these years," Janet said. "I remember thinking, *If I did have a dad, I'd want him to be a man like Chuck.*" For all those years, he was.

YOUR JOURNEY

Exploring Your Story

1. In what ways is your story the same as Janet's? In what ways is it different?

2. When you feel rejected, do you tend to deal with it internally — low self-esteem, self-doubt? Or externally — anger, hostility toward others, withdrawal?

3. With regard to your experience of rejection, where would you place yourself on the journey toward healing?

Exploring God's Word

1. Read Gen. 16. Would you say that Hagar was partly responsible for her own situation? Why or why not?

2. How do you think Hagar may have felt when she realized that God knew all about

her situation?

3. What experiences make you feel that God knows and cares about you?

Exploring the Steps to Healing

1. Of the steps to healing listed in this chapter, which have you already taken, and which have you yet to take?

2. Does bitterness feel like something you're stuck with? Have you tried letting go of it?

3. What would it take for you to forgive the person(s) who rejected you?

5
FAILURE
FROM REMORSE TO GRACE

Point of Healing
I have the courage to try again because
I know that God forgives me when I fail.

It is a great art to laugh at one's own
misfortune.
— Danish proverb

Mark Evans looked at the new sign outside
his downtown office and grinned like a six-
year-old. Computer Services, Ltd. "We
made it, Jeff," he said gleefully.

"We sure did, partner," said Jeff Helton.
"We're in the big time now."

Mark had dreamed of this moment his
whole life. He remembered the days of ped-
dling newspapers in his Minnesota home-
town. *Someday, I'll have my own business.*
He remembered his first job at Digital
Services in Rochester, where he had met

Jeff. One a software engineer, the other a salesman, they had formed an unlikely friendship. After just six months on the job, Mark discovered a process improvement that saved the company more in two weeks than he earned in a year. *I could run this place,* he thought. *All I need is a start.*

And he remembered that table at Starbucks, the one next to the window overlooking Sixth Street. That's where his pipe dream became reality over a warm scone and a cup of hot cappuccino. Mark had an idea for a unique electronic delivery service. Jeff had a contact in the finance industry. They had the idea and the money. The dream became reality.

"It was right there in my hands," Mark recalls. "I had a state-of-the-art product. I had financial backing. There were no roadblocks."

Business was hot for nearly two years as clients practically waited in line to buy their service. But success proved to be challenging. "It's weird," Mark recalls. "We were bringing in more money than I'd ever seen before, but we were always broke. We were expanding so fast that we needed more capital nearly every month."

They added support staff. They hired a marketing firm. They started a research and development team. Each expansion brought new excitement, but there was a price. "It costs a lot to stay on the cutting edge," Mark says. "I had no idea what the payback for that growth would be."

Mark and Jeff soon outgrew their older, downtown office and moved to a sprawling complex in suburban Minneapolis. The offices of Computer Services, Ltd. were a hectic but happy place. "I really thought everything was fine," Mark says. "I was zoned-in on developing new product, and that's what I'm best at. I was president of the company, but I never thought much about the venture capital loans. I figured that was Jeff's responsibility."

It was a Wednesday morning when Scott Osmond called. Mark rarely spoke with the president of Venture Corp., so the lunch invitation came as a surprise. "Sure, I can meet," Mark said hesitantly. "Is 12:30 OK?"

Two hours later Mark greeted the young entrepreneur, who now held a majority interest in the company. Mark's partner, Jeff, wasn't able to attend.

Easy banter graced the Caesar salad and mineral water in the upscale suburban restaurant. After lunch Mark ordered a latte. Then Scott Osmond changed the subject abruptly.

"Mark, we need to make a change."

"Change?" Mark felt the chill. "Things are great. What would we change?"

Scott's eyes narrowed. "We're moving a specialist in to take charge of the company."

"The company?" Mark responded. "You mean *my* company? You want someone to take charge of my company?"

Before Scott answered, Mark saw the handwriting on the wall. The dream of financial independence was turning to a nightmare — with elevator music playing in the background. They had hit the big time all right, but they were way beyond their league. In a flash, it all made sense — the hasty borrowing, the quarterly financial goals that they had barely missed, the warning messages from accounting.

"I'm sorry, Mark. The numbers just aren't there. We've crunched them several times. The debt load is just too great. We're putting Fred Anderson in the front office of the company. He's had years of experience."

"In computer services?" Mark quizzed.

"No, Mark. In business. Computer Services, Ltd. is not a software lab. It's a commercial enterprise. We need a business person at the top."

The words cut Mark to the heart. "This was my dream," Mark stammered. "My

111

partner and I built this company from the ground up, and now you're bringing in somebody who doesn't even know what we do."

Suddenly Mark thought of a more immediate concern. He looked up from the table. "What about me, Scott? What do I do now?"

"I'd like you to stay on as a consultant," the investor responded. "We'll need your experience — and your relationship with the clients."

You've got to be kidding, Mark thought. *I hired this staff. I'm their boss. Now this pencil pusher wants me to punch the clock right along with them.*

Scott started to speak but stopped himself, as if unsure whether to say more. Slowly, he said, "Mark, I hate to say this, but you're not a leader. You're a software engineer, and you're a good one. Maybe if you'd been a little smarter about the numbers . . . Look, I really hope you'll stay on. The company needs your expertise."

Mark stared out the window, his mind racing. He tried to imagine making the announcement to his staff. *Anybody got a spare cubicle?* He wondered what his wife's reaction would be. *How could you be so stupid?* How would he tell his children? *Hey, kids, your loser dad is home.* He pictured himself walking back in to Digital Services and submitting a résumé. *All our current openings are entry level.* Could he bear that humiliation?

I wish I could just disappear, Mark thought. *I want to make it all go away.*

"So what do you say, Mark? Can we count on you?"

"I'll have to think about it," Mark answered slowly. "I've got some decisions to make."

THE EFFECT OF FAILURE

There are two ways to fail, on the inside and on the outside. People who fail on the outside shoot for something big and miss. They attempt to sail around the world but make it only as far as Borneo. They try out for the basketball team but get cut in the second round. They try to merge their successful business with another to corner the market on widgets, but the economy goes bad and they lose it all. They fail because they dared too much and thought too little. They bit off more than they could chew.

There's another way to fail, and that's from the inside. People who fail this way don't meet external roadblocks — they succumb to internal pressures. The fault, as

113

Shakespeare put it, lies not in the world but in themselves. They fail because they give way to the private temptation of fear, lust, or laziness. The world would have allowed them to succeed, but they wouldn't allow it themselves. They fail in their work because they lack the discipline to apply themselves. They fail in business because they are naively overconfident. They fail as leaders because they lack the courage to make tough decisions. They fail as spouses because they lack the self-confidence to say no.

Failure from either direction is devastating. From whatever source, failure gives rise to a sickening self-contempt. Defeated, discouraged, demoralized, those who have failed experience a series of emotions that are unknown to those whose enemies come from without.

Shame

Shame is the first by-product of failure. When we fail, we see ourselves as limited, helpless, sinful, weak. It's not a pretty sight. We don't visualize our picture on the cover of *Time* magazine. Those who have failed seldom need anyone to point out their shortcomings. They recite them for themselves: *I'm an idiot. I should have checked the stock report. The deadline was printed on the application.*

Those who have failed are offered a fresh version of one of Satan's oldest lies — everybody's better than you. And the lie is often believed.

Remorse

"I knew it was my fault," Mark laments. "For weeks I rehearsed the details of the past two years, agonizing over the things I should have done differently."

Failure always has a personal element. *I was selfish. I got lazy. I didn't pay attention. I should have known better.*

Often we feel remorse because we're responsible — and we know it.

Even when others are partly responsible, we blame ourselves. *I had it coming.* Whether that's true or not, the feeling is common to those whose dreams died on the doorstep.

Self-contempt

Those who fail blame themselves. Judas, who betrayed Christ, was so consumed by remorse that he took his own life (see Matt. 27:1–10). He's not alone. The sidewalks of Wall Street ran red with the blood of failed investors who leaped to their deaths after the crash of the Great Depression. Remorse mixed with fear is a lethal combination.

In some cases, the path to self-destruction is less obvious. Self-hatred can be the driving force behind substance abuse, sexual addiction, or extreme living. We work or play ourselves to death because we value our lives too little.

Resentment

Failure changes lives, sometimes for keeps. Jobs are lost. Marriages are dissolved. Savings are depleted. Reputations are ruined. Each failure has a price tag.

Failure brings loss, and loss brings resentment. When your life changes dramatically for the worse, it seems unfair that others go on with business as usual. Anger gives rise to spiteful thoughts. *I should be living in that house. That income should be mine. Those people don't deserve what they have.*

"I was making over $100,000 a year," Mark recalls, "and that was just salary. Add up the perks and bonuses, and the total was much higher." His income dropped to zero in five minutes. "Don't think I wasn't bitter."

Paralysis

A 2002 study by Carnegie Mellon University shows that after the September 11,

2001, attacks, 20 percent of Americans believed they could be hurt in a terrorist attack sometime during the next year. In fact, the number of people injured in terrorist attacks was quite small compared to other sources of injury. Far more people are injured in home accidents than by terrorists.[1] Yet the *fear* of terrorism significantly affected the American way of life as many people refused to travel, invest money, or make significant purchases.

Those who have failed often suffer a similar paralysis. Failure breeds the fear of failure. We pull back from relationships. We withdraw emotionally. We become unwilling to risk. We hoard our resources. We philosophize: "Fool me once — shame on you; fool me twice — shame on me." *Why venture out?* we figure. *It's dangerous out there. I have the scars to prove it!*

There's an interesting parallel in the Bible.

GOD'S WORD

"No way, Lord. Even if everyone else turns coward, I never will. I'll never let you down." That boast set up one of the greatest failures in Scripture — Peter's denial of Christ. The story unfolds in Matt. 26.

Gathering His disciples for their last supper together, Jesus surprised the loyal band of followers with two stunning predictions. "First," Jesus said, "one of you will betray Me. What's more, all of you will desert Me in the end."

The bombastic apostle, always ready for an argument, spoke up boldly. "Even if all fall away on account of you," Peter protested, "I never will" (v. 33).

In spite of Peter's affirmation of loyalty, Jesus reiterated His prediction. "This very night, before the rooster crows, you will disown me three times" (v. 34).

This made Peter more determined than ever. "Even if I have to die with you," he insisted, "I will never disown you" (v. 35). And he meant it. A few hours later, the disciples were asleep in the Garden of Gethsemane; Jesus was praying nearby. Suddenly a band of soldiers appeared, led by Judas the betrayer. As they seized Jesus, Peter drew a sword and attacked, albeit ineptly. He succeeded only in cutting off the ear of one of the servants (John 18:10). He had sworn to stand by Jesus, and he was ready to keep his word.

As the night wore on, however, Peter's confidence wavered. Within hours, Jesus was on trial for blasphemy before the Sanhedrin, the council of Jewish religious leaders.

A conviction there would almost certainly bring a death sentence, sure to be enforced by the Roman civil government.

A crowd of curious onlookers waited in the courtyard. Peter, realizing that public opinion was turning against Jesus, became worried about the outcome. He crouched to warm himself by the fire and listen for any news. Seeing his face in the flickering firelight, a servant girl recognized Peter as a follower of Jesus. "You were with Him," she said simply.

Peter froze. "You're mistaken," he mumbled and moved away from the fire.

Standing near the gate, another girl recognized him. "You're one of them," she said. "You were with that man from Nazareth."

Peter slid into the shadows. "No," he said emphatically. "You've got the wrong man."

Now there was a buzz in the crowd. They began whispering, gesturing in Peter's direction. Finally a group of them approached him. One of them said, "I know you're one of them. Your accent gives you away. You're from Galilee."

In a panic Peter denied it a third time, cursing and shouting, "I tell you — I don't know the man!"

At that moment a rooster crowed. Peter remembered Jesus' prediction. He had deserted Jesus at last. He slipped outside the gate into the darkness and hurled himself to the ground, weeping bitterly.

Everyone Fails

Peter is not alone in having failed. Many outstanding people have borne the heavy chains of failure before wearing the lofty ribbons of success. Abraham Lincoln was a defeated congressional candidate before he was president. Albert Einstein was a rejected college applicant before he was the celebrated scientist. Baseball great Hank Aaron went 0–5 in his rookie major league start. Starting poorly doesn't mean you won't finish well. Nearly everyone fails at some time or another.

Peter's personal tragedy illustrates for us the truth that every human being is susceptible to failure.

Failure does not result from being different but from being the same as everyone else. There's no upper class of people for whom failure is foreign. Everyone does it. We fail because we're human.

And failure is not always the result of moral weakness. Peter's failure was a failure of courage, a failure of judgment. He did not betray Jesus for money, as Judas did. He simply underestimated the situation. He judged the circumstances — and himself — poorly.

Most of our failures are the result of poor judgment, not character flaws. We borrow more than we should. We're inattentive. We're to blame for these errors in judgment, but they don't necessarily indicate character flaws.

There Is Grace for Those Who Fail

Peter's story does not end on the night of Jesus' trial. Unlike Judas, who hanged himself in a fit of remorse (Matt. 27:5), Peter crept back into the circle of Jesus' disciples. And when Jesus appeared to some women after His resurrection, He instructed them specifically to tell Peter that He was alive (Mark 16:7). Later, when the two were reunited on the shores of the Sea of Galilee, Jesus reinstated Peter to his position of leadership among the Twelve (see John 21:15–19). Peter wasn't finished with Jesus, and Jesus wasn't finished with Peter. Failure did not spell the end of his usefulness as a disciple. In fact, it became his turning point.

Grace always overcomes failure. God graciously forgives our sin. Others are most often gracious in forgiving our failures. Henry F. Lyte reminds us that God himself puts the finishing strokes to the portrait of our lives:

> *Fatherlike, He tends and spares us;*
> *well our feeble frame He knows.*
> *In His hands He gently bears us,*
> *rescues us from all our foes.*
> *Alleluia! Alleluia!*
> *widely yet His mercy flows.*[2]

There Is Life After Failure

Jesus predicted that Peter would become "the rock" upon which the Church would be built (Matt. 16:18). In spite of his humiliating failure in the courtyard, Peter did rise to become the leader of the Early Church, first in Jerusalem and later in Rome.

And failure along the way doesn't mean you're through. On April 14, 2000, Wall Street suffered the biggest one-day loss in United States financial history. Investors lost an estimated $2 trillion. Bill Gates, the chairman of Microsoft, saw his personal fortune drop a staggering $30 billion in a matter of hours. But not all was lost. Mr. Gates continues to be quite wealthy. It's estimated even after that loss, his personal fortune was worth more $46 billion.[3] Obviously, failure need not be fatal.

Like Bill Gates, you'll find that what remains is nearly always greater than what was lost. That fortune will likely not be in billion-dollar leftovers. It will be in something of even greater worth: grace. God gives us the spiritual capital to rise above failure. That's the point of the gospel, in fact. We're free from slavery to the past, free to rise up, free to try again, free to succeed. The apostle Paul reminds us that "God is able to make all grace abound to you, so that in all things at all times, having all that you need, you will abound in every good work" (2 Cor. 9:8).

It's true. He did that for Peter. He'll do it for you.

STEPS TO HEALING

It takes courage to move beyond failure. It takes courage to accept the loss, admit the truth, and move on. That's the courage that Peter had when he got up from the ground and made his way back to Christ. Every recovery from failure begins with the same decision, the decision to look ahead. Here are some steps that begin the journey from failure to joy.

Admit the Truth

"For months I blamed Scott Osmond for

taking my business," Mark says. "It took me a long time to admit that *I* lost my business."

Some failures result from character weakness, wrongdoing, or neglect. If yours does, face it. Deal openly with your shortcomings. Blaming others, denying the reality of your situation, or minimizing your own shortcomings will not enable you to succeed. You must face the present in order to reach the future.

Accept Grace

God will forgive you for failing, and others may forgive you for letting them down. But you must let them. Accepting grace implies an admission of failure — you must agree that you failed. Admit it. Then accept the help that God and others will gladly offer. Failure does not make you a second-class person. Everyone has failed to live up to God's perfect standard for living. The Bible says that "all have sinned and fall short of the glory of God" (Rom. 3:23). The good news is that God always offers the opportunity to begin again.

Determine to Change

"I know I didn't pay attention to business," Mark says. "I had a good idea, and I let it go to my head. That's a mistake I won't make again." Mark turned the mistakes into milestones, places of learning. The curve in the road became a learning curve when he determined to make changes in his leadership style. He studied. He observed others. He examined his business methods microscopically.

You'll have to do the same drill.

- What factors made you susceptible to temptation?

- What personal shortcomings hindered your success in business?

- How might you have contributed to the problems in your marriage?

You must be willing to do something different from what you're doing now in order to make a change. Are you where you want to be in life? What needs to change to get you there?

Make Lifestyle Adjustments

Be realistic about your circumstances. You can't continue living on a $100,000 annual income if you're now bringing home $300 a week. You may need to make hard choices.

Recognize the changes that have come

into your life — and those that will come. Understand that you can still be well dressed without designer clothes. You can get from point A to point B without a luxury automobile.

Change may be needed in other areas as well. What was lost when you failed? Job? Position? Income? Relationships? Trust? Be willing to make the changes necessary to deal with that loss. Your future depends upon it.

Accept Help

"After I lost the business, I avoided seeing people," Mark reports. Too bad. It was those same people who would eventually help him get back on his feet.

Sometimes it's hard to accept help, but it may be necessary. You've lent a hand to others before. Now it's your turn. Remember the speech you gave to that friend or loved one when you stood alongside him or her in adversity? "You'd do the same thing for me." Now it's their turn to share in the blessing of giving.

Be Patient

Recovery takes time. That's true in every area of life — physical, emotional, financial. It takes time to pay debts, mend relationships, learn new skills, change careers, build trust. Forgiveness can come in an instant. Recovery takes longer. One year is generally not a sufficient length of time to recover from a life trauma. Rebuilding your life after a failed marriage, lost career, or financial wipeout may take years, not weeks. Set realistic goals, and work patiently toward them.

Try Again

The most dangerous result of failure is the feeling of worthlessness. If you believe you can't, you won't. If you're convinced there's no point, you'll never try. Believe that you can succeed. Understand that God wants your success — in life, in business, in marriage.

People don't become failures because they fall down. They become failures because they *stay* down. Get up and try again.

THE POINT OF HEALING

"Maybe I should take the consulting position," Mark wondered aloud. He and Jeff sat in a half-empty McDonald's, sipping coffee and wondering about their uncertain futures. Jeff, it turned out, had also been offered a token position.

"No," Jeff said bitterly. "I think we need

to let it go."

And it went. Within weeks, the team Mark had assembled bailed out on the new management. The new president's scant understanding of the computer industry made clients nervous. Within a few months Computer Services, Ltd., was out of business.

"After 10 years of hard work, I was out on the street with nothing," Mark recalls. "I was down to one month of paid health insurance and had nothing but a mountain of debt." Mark sold his home and most of the family's belongings in order to pay bills and was looking desperately for a place to live. "I think the low point came when I was turned down for a low-rent apartment. We wound up living in the basement of a friend's house."

The worst problem, however, was spiritual, not financial. The faith that had been so integral to Mark's life seemed to have deserted him. "I was hurt. I was disappointed. I was angry," Mark recalls. "There wasn't anything to lean on. I couldn't lean on my self — doing that had blown up in my face. I had no money and no job prospects. I had no idea what to do."

Alone in his friend's basement, wallowing in self-pity, Mark reached a breaking point. "I could only think of one thing to do. I began to cry out to God."

God answered.

"Mark! There's someone here to see you," his wife called through the basement doorway.

"I'll be right up."

Jack Sorenson, a friend from church, stood at the front door. "Carol and I have been praying for you and your family," he said, placing an envelope in Mark's hand. "We know you've been through some difficult times. We want to help."

Without waiting for a response, Jack added, "God bless you guys," and turned back toward the car that sat idling in the driveway.

Mark took the envelope downstairs. Sitting at the small kitchen table, he opened it to find a check for $5,000.

"I began to cry like a baby," Mark admits. "A few minutes earlier I had been lamenting the fact that I couldn't provide for my family and cried out to God for help — then this." Mark didn't get much sleep that night. He spent most of it lying awake and praising God.

Within a week, another friend called from his cell phone while driving to meet a client in his new Mercedes. "How's business?" he asked, and Mark quickly brought him up to date.

"What are you going to do now?" the friend inquired.

"I don't have a clue," Mark answered.

"Hold on," he said, as he put the cell phone down and maneuvered his car to the side of the road. "We're going to pray about this right now."

"As he prayed," Mark says, "it was like electricity running through me. The presence of God was so real. I had goose bumps so big you could have hung a hat on them. It was like a second wave. God was telling me that everything was under control."

"I was OK after that," Mark recalls. "I began to heal that day — emotionally, financially, and spiritually. Each new day was a step of faith. We had months, actually years, of financial struggles ahead of us. But that was the day my heart turned around. I knew that God would provide for us."

Within a few months, Mark began to do some consulting work with the friends he met through his part-time job. Mark now has a successful new career. His failure is past. His future is alive with God's promises.

So is yours — if you believe it.

Exploring Your Story

1. In what ways is your story like Mark's? In what ways is it different?

2. Which aspects of your failure were the fault of others? For which were you responsible?

3. Describe the effects of your experience on your personal, spiritual, family, and financial life.

Exploring God's Word

1. Read Matt. 26. Why do you think Jesus chose the disciples He did, given the fact that one would betray Him and all would desert Him?

2. Compare and contrast the actions of Judas and Peter and their responses to their respective failures.

3. Read John 21:15−19. Do you think Jesus and Peter were fully reconciled? Why or why not?

Exploring the Steps to Healing

1. In what ways have you taken responsibility for your failure?

2. Of the steps to healing listed in this chapter, which have you already taken? Which have you yet to take?

3. Spend some time with a mature

Christian who knows you well. Ask him or her to analyze your abilities and temperament, listing your five greatest strengths and three areas in which you need improvement.

6
Pain
FROM DOUBT TO TRUST

Point of Healing
I will patiently endure because I know
that God is in control of my life.

If I were to say, "God, why me?" about
the bad things, then I should have said,
"God, why me?" about the good things
that happened in my life.
— Arthur Ashe

"Pastor, that's the best sermon on grace I've ever heard."

The young minister smiled appreciatively. "Thanks, Martin. And it's true," he added, referring to 2 Cor. 12:9. "God's grace *is* sufficient for every situation." Within minutes, Brian Snyder's belief in the God of grace would be put to a test, one that would last for the rest of his life.

Brian had just completed a preaching assignment at a church in rural New York state. Shortly after noon, he pulled out of the church parking lot and headed east on Route 374. Three minutes later, a westbound vehicle veered across the center line.

The state trooper who investigated the crash estimated the force of impact at more than 100 miles per hour. There were no skid marks. The near-head-on collision jolted Brian's car into a cornfield, where it rolled three times.

O God, I'm dying! he cried as flames appeared in the rear of the car.

It's OK, God seemed to say through the terror and confusion. *I'll be with you.* Brian felt comforted, even though his hips were badly crushed and he was bleeding from injuries to the head and chest. He lost consciousness just as the rescue team arrived at the scene.

"Brian is alive," the surgeon announced to the young man's family. Rescuers had extracted Brian's broken body from the wreck and transported him to the medical center in Plattsburgh. After nine hours of surgery, his bones had been set, but his body was far from whole. "Fortunately, he wasn't burned, but his pelvis was badly damaged," the doctor said. "If he survives, he may never walk again."

Three days later, Brian began to wake from a drug-induced coma and realized how badly he was injured. "I couldn't eat," he recalls. "I couldn't walk. I couldn't even pray. But Ps. 34:7 came into my mind, and I began to quote it over and over: 'The angel of the LORD encamps around those who fear him, and he delivers them.' "

On the sixth day after his accident, Brian received a special visitor. God sent an angel to comfort him. "It was two o'clock in the morning. Suddenly the room was filled with an unusual brightness. I looked up and saw the form of a little child. I believe that God sent a ministering angel to my room." That night, Brian found the strength to begin his arduous recovery. He felt at peace, energized. Friends remarked on how well he was coping with the trauma.

Then the pain came — searing pain from the surgical wounds, throbbing pain from broken bones, aching pain from a damaged sciatic nerve, constant pain from sitting or lying still for too long. There were headaches, back pain, pain from wounded limbs, and pain from the muscles and joints that had to compensate for the others. "I had pain in nearly every part of my body," Brian remembers. "Even with medication, the pain was unbearable."

After three months of endless therapy and relentless pain, Brian's spirit broke. His wife, Sheila, noticed a change in his attitude. While driving to yet another medical appointment, she asked, "Honey, are you OK?"

"I just don't understand why this had to happen to me," Brian said bitterly. "What did I do to deserve this?"

"I — I don't know."

"How could God do this to me?" Brian demanded.

"Honey, I don't think God would —"

"Don't tell me what God would do. I *know* what He did."

They spent the rest of the drive in silence, Sheila silently praying for her husband's faith, Brian silently questioning God.

As he hobbled out of the doctor's office, fighting to maneuver his crutches into the car, Sheila offered a suggestion. "Brian, Nancy Heller called again yesterday." The managing editor for *New Life* magazine had been in college with Brian and was keeping tabs on the family during his recovery. "She wondered if you might be feeling well enough to take a writing assignment — a short article, on grace. Maybe it would help to have something to do."

"I don't think so," Brian responded,

clutching a new prescription for pain medication.

"Well, I think she was just trying to help."

Brian closed the car door, wincing at the pain in his hips and back. "I know," he said, gritting his teeth. "But I don't have much to say about God right now. And I'm not sure if I ever will."

THE EFFECT OF PAIN

During the first days after his accident, Brian's faith held up well. He remembered scripture. He was encouraged by friends. He even received a visit from an angel. Although his life had been radically altered, he was accepting, at peace.

Pain changed that. Daily, unrelenting, unmerciful pain caused him to doubt.

Brian's experience is typical. The slow burn of pain, the long days — even years — of living with discomfort and enduring quiet misery is the greatest challenge to our belief in a gracious God.

That doubt can arise from what might seem to others like minor discomfort. The nagging ache of arthritis, the predictable discomfort of premenstrual syndrome, the occasional blinding pain of migraine headaches — any of these so-called routine conditions can bring troublesome, consistent, even intense pain and the doubt that often accompanies them.

According to the National Institute of Neurological Disorders and Stroke, some 90 million Americans suffer from chronic pain.[1] More than 1,200,000 new cases of cancer are reported each year, and most victims suffer chronic pain. Arthritis pain affects more than 40 million Americans each year, and as many as 45 million Americans have chronic, severe headaches. Migraine sufferers account for more than 157 million lost workdays each year.[2]

Pain has a predictable effect on the spirit. Researchers refer to the condition as the "terrible triad" of suffering, sleeplessness, and sadness.[3] Chronic pain may produce side effects like the following.

Anger

Why me? Why did this have to happen to me? What did I do to deserve this?

For those suffering physically, especially if it involves pain, these questions are natural. But they belie a dangerous attitude, one that says, *This shouldn't have happened to me. My life was supposed to be different.*

Doubt

Anger often gives way to an even more

troubling problem — doubt. Pain is different from some other forms of life trauma in that it focuses attention squarely on God. When we suffer pain, we usually don't blame our spouses, kids, or friends. They're obviously not responsible. God is the culprit, we figure. He could have prevented our suffering but chose not to. If God is good, we ask, then why am I suffering? In fact, if God is good, then why does anyone suffer?

Irritability

Many older people suffer pain from arthritis and other chronic ailments. Dealing with constant pain and the accompanying physical limitations can cause them to be a pain to others. By some estimates, 86 percent of elderly people have at least one chronic illness that can be painful.[4]

Pain causes us to focus on ourselves. Partly, that's because pain is the signaling mechanism that God placed in our bodies to indicate there's a problem. When we feel it, we're supposed to slow down and figure out what's wrong.

Over time, however, some pain sufferers replace a healthy attention to personal needs with outright selfishness. We demand our own way and become impatient with those trying to help us. A veneer of politeness will not last long in the presence of pain. It will reveal the selfishness that lies beneath the surface.

Apathy

Pain holds the body hostage. Going out is torturous, so you stay in. Movement is irritating, so you sit or lie down. Interaction with others requires energy, so you withdraw. Soon it becomes difficult to believe that a "normal" life is possible.

Despair

Pain brings loss of mobility, loss of function, loss of opportunity, and sometimes loss of relationships. Grief accompanies every loss, including the loss of normalcy.

Because of the pain, sufferers at first fear they may die. But when pain is too intense or lasts too long, they fear they may not. Death is seen as a release from a pain-riddled life.

What happens when the pain just won't go away? Can life be normal in spite of pain? The answer is yes. God's Word speaks of a treatment for pain that works not on the body but on the soul. It's called *faith*.

GOD'S WORD

He was living the American dream. At

midlife he was wealthy and had the good health to enjoy it. He had raised a large family, all of them doing well, and was an empty nester, just beginning to enjoy the best years of his life. He had a successful career, a fine home, and the freedom to travel. Now he would really enjoy life.

Then the phone rang. "Your children were on a cruise in the Mediterranean. Terrorists hijacked the ship. The rescue effort failed. They were all killed."

Minutes later, the television blared the headline news. "The stock market took a beating today. Technology stocks were hard hit. Micromerge was wiped out." He had lost everything.

Finally, the claims adjustor delivered a hopeless report. "It was a case of arson. Your home was completely destroyed. Your assistant failed to renew your coverage. Everything is gone."

A version of that incredible story is found in the oldest book of the Bible, Job. Job was one of the wealthiest men of his day and one of the most faithful. For that very reason, Satan asked God's permission to test Job in order to find out if suffering would affect his steady faith. "Sure, Job worships you," Satan scoffed. "He's got it made. Why wouldn't he be faithful? Take away his good life, and his faith will crumble."

Then, in one of the most puzzling events in Scripture, God entered into something like a wager with Satan. "Go ahead," God said. "Do your worst to Job." And Satan did, wiping out Job's family, his home, and all his wealth in a single day. Later, Satan was allowed to inflict illness on Job, and he suffered intense pain from boils that covered his body. Through all of this, Job remained faithful to God. "Though he slay me," Job said, "yet will I hope in him" (13:15).

How did he do it?

He Looked to God, Not Himself

First, Job looked to God, not himself. When he received the news that his family and wealth had been destroyed, his response was immediate. "At this, Job got up and tore his robe and shaved his head. Then he fell to the ground in worship and said: 'Naked I came from my mother's womb, and naked I will depart. The LORD gave and the LORD has taken away; may the name of the LORD be praised" (Job 1:20–21).

Job's first thought was not of himself and what he had lost. His first thought was to seek God and to honor Him. He saw all these things — wealth, family, possessions, and even health — as gifts, not rights.

It's interesting that Brian had a similar response. In his first moments of consciousness after surgery, he thought of scripture, reciting God's Word as an affirmation.

He Refused to Blame God

Job also refused to blame God. Not only were Job's circumstances intolerable, but those people who might have encouraged him actually attacked his faith even further. Job's wife offered this advice: "Curse God and die!" (2:9). Harsh words, but most of us think along similar lines when attacked by pain — it's God's fault. And when pain becomes severe, sufferers prefer even death to pain.

Yet Job, in spite of his suffering, was able to see his situation clearly. He cut to the bottom line with a response that forms the classic Christian understanding of good and evil. He asked, "Shall we accept good from God, and not trouble?" (2:10).

Job understood that since God could prevent our suffering but chooses not to, He is ultimately responsible for it. The interplay between Satan and God in this story illustrates that truth. It was Satan who inflicted suffering on Job, but with God's permission. Satan could not have harmed Job unless God allowed it, but God did not actively inflict Job's pain. He allowed suffering for a reason. A parent who allows a child to go outside without a coat makes a similar choice. The parent knows that Junior will soon be cold and uncomfortable, but Mom or Dad allows that "pain" for a greater reason — to teach responsibility. Does that make for a bad parent? Hardly.

In the same way, God is still good, even when our circumstances aren't. He allows our suffering for a reason — one that may not be immediately apparent to us. And as it was with Job, the pain we suffer becomes a test of our faith as we're forced to make an excruciating choice — to believe that God is good in spite of our own suffering.

Job made that affirmation. Scripture records that "in all this, Job did not sin by charging God with wrongdoing" (1:22).

He Refused Bad Advice

Job's wife was not the only one to pour salt on his wounds. Soon three friends came by to comfort him. Their comfort consisted mostly of berating Job for being prideful. They believed that he must be guilty of some sin, otherwise God surely would not have punished him by inflicting pain. Obviously, they reasoned, Job was being prideful by not admitting that he had done something wrong.

It is true that all suffering is the result of sin. Adam's original sin brought death into the world (see Gen. 3). Since then, we have carried on the grand tradition — we all have sinned and all suffer under the curse of death that God placed on the world.

It is not true, however, that each instance of suffering is the result of some individual wrongdoing. In other words, God doesn't punish us for individual sins by inflicting illness or pain. Jesus made that clear when His disciples noticed a man who had been blind since birth and asked, "Who sinned, this man or his parents, that he was born blind?" Jesus said, "Neither this man nor his parents sinned, . . . but this happened so that the work of God might be displayed in his life" (John 9:2–3). Yet God does use pain as a means to bring glory to himself. Job understood that.

He Expressed Himself Honestly

Job was not afraid to ask hard questions or say things that are difficult to hear. He was candid first about his own situation. "I will speak out in the anguish of my spirit," he said, "I will complain in the bitterness of my soul" (7:11). He lamented his situation, even wishing that he had never been born, and wondered aloud what every pain-sufferer has wondered: *Why?* He proved that it's possible to question God without disbelieving, an important distinction for pain-sufferers. Asking "Why did this happen to me" is different from "Why did You do this to me?" One is a request for insight, the other an accusation.

He Accepted His Suffering

Finally, after lengthy speeches by both Job and his friends, the only person with all the answers — God — spoke. But He did not answer any of Job's questions or provide any explanation for his pain. Instead, God chided Job for speaking about things he didn't understand. "Who is this that darkens my counsel with words without knowledge?" God asked. "Brace yourself like a man; I will question you, and you shall answer me. Where were you when I laid the earth's foundation?" (38:2–4). Since you know nothing about how the world works, God was saying, you can't understand the reasons you suffer.

God might answer our questions in a similar, though hopefully less dramatic, way. Why do you experience chronic pain? Perhaps you won't know the answer to that question. What good is accomplished by your suffering? God may never reveal that to you. Unfair? From our limited perspective, it seems so. But from God's vantage point — overlooking all of the world, all of time, all of eternity — His actions make perfect sense.

After a number of withering questions from God, Job answered humbly, "Surely I spoke of things I did not understand, things too wonderful for me to know" (42:3). Job realized that it was futile to question God, for he would be unable to understand God's answers even if they were given. In the end, Job chose to combine two seemingly contradictory actions. He both accepted his suffering and affirmed that God is good.

STEPS TO HEALING

Unfortunately, it's not always possible to remove pain. Many sufferers must find a way to be spiritually whole in spite of ongoing discomfort. They must, in effect, fight against two diseases at the same time: physical pain and the spiritual pain that it produces. It's a tremendous challenge.

Yet it can be met. Job is not our only example of faith through suffering. The apostle Paul endured a thorn in the flesh, yet he remained faithful, even optimistic. Christ endured the agony of crucifixion and, even while hanging on the Cross, prayed forgiveness for His torturers. It is possible to be spiritually whole in a broken body. The following are some steps toward healing.

Believe That God Is Good

Faith, as the Bible reminds us, is being sure of what we do not see (Heb. 11:1). When you're suffering, it's difficult to believe that God is good. But He is. Pain is perhaps the most personal manifestation of evil. Those who endure it are faced with one of life's hardest questions on a daily basis: If God is good, then why do bad things happen — to *me?*

There is no easy answer, but there are principles that inform us. Human suffering is a result of the human sin that began with the first human pair. God allows our suffering, which is different from inflicting it, and God frequently teaches us lessons through pain. All these things are true. Yet they are cold comfort to those whose bodies are aching. In the end, we're left with contradictory truths. God *is* good, and He *does* allow our suffering.

The road to healing begins with the affirmation that, in spite of what we suffer, God can be trusted. He knows you hurt, and He cares. In spite of the pain, He continues to have your best interests at heart. Trust Him. He won't let you down.

Forgive Those Who Have Hurt You

Some suffering results from illness; the cause can be difficult to identify. Other suffering sometimes results from human wrongdoing. If you suffer pain because of an injury, you may know the cause — by name! It may be true that what you don't know can't hurt you, but some scientists have proven that *who* you know can. The *San Francisco Chronicle* reported on a 2002 study that provides clues to the origin of chronic pain. Researchers found that "early life experiences and social factors — even the mere presence of an overly solicitous spouse — can make the problem worse."[5]

Resentment, bitterness, or unforgiveness may be a contributor to what ails you. Forgive those who have caused you pain, for your sake.

Focus on the Eternal

Many people are preoccupied with their own bodies — their beauty, their physical fitness. And pain sufferers can become obsessed with their own comfort. All three have this in common: they have shifted the focus from eternal things, which really matter, to temporary things, which really don't.

The apostle Paul summarizes the situation perfectly. After rehearsing a litany of his own sufferings, everything from enduring shipwreck to physical beatings, he offers this sage advice:

> Therefore we do not lose heart. Though outwardly we are wasting away, yet inwardly we are being renewed day by day. For our light and momentary troubles are achieving for us an eternal glory that far outweighs them all. So we fix our eyes not on what is seen, but on what is unseen. For what is seen is temporary, but what is unseen is eternal *(2 Cor. 4:16–18)*.

Your body won't last forever. It wasn't meant to. Yes, you are getting weaker, more susceptible to infirmity, and you therefore suffer more pain. That's true for every human, whether or not he or she knows it. Our challenge is to remember that amid this often-painful life, we have the hope of something better. Look to the future — not the day after tomorrow, but eternity.

Find a Focus
Finding a focus for mental and physical

energy is an aid to coping with pain. "I learned to focus on my work," Brian Snyder says. "I have hobbies. I stay busy." Having a purposeful activity gives you something better than a narcotic: a reason to keep going. On a practical level, work or some other meaningful activity is one of the best antidotes to the trauma inflicted by pain.

- Go to work every day you can. It will keep your mind focused on something besides yourself.

- Develop friendships. They will keep you from feeling lonely.

- Garden, work with wood, or read. It will keep you connected with the world outside.

- Do something productive. It will keep you from feeling useless.

Manage the Physical Symptoms

Pain sufferers do themselves no spiritual service by ignoring medical aid. If you suffer physical symptoms, seek the care of a physician, and follow his or her advice. Being brave is not a badge of courage or independence. Care for your body as best you can.

Communicate with Family and Friends

Sufferers often close themselves behind a wall of withdrawal. "Nobody understands," they reason. "It does no good to talk about how I feel."

It's true that few may understand the agony of ongoing pain. But those around you need to understand what you're experiencing and how it affects your life. Don't agree to a task that's overly demanding when the result is unbearable pain.

Tell loved ones what your limits are. Let them know what would help you the most. And listen. Communication is a two-way street. Find out what you can do to make their lives easier. Be understanding of how your pain affects those around you.

Pray

Jesus understands your suffering. He suffered, just as you do, and even more. He understands, and He cares. Talk with Him. He is your constant companion and friend.

When American prisoner of war Jessica Lynch was rescued from an Iraqi hospital that had been converted to a prison for American soldiers, a rescuer approached her hospital bed with these welcome words: "Jessica Lynch! We are United States soldiers, and we're here to protect you and take you home." The frightened private reached out her hand and begged, "Please, don't anybody leave me."[7]

When you're suffering pain, God won't leave you. He'll call you by name, come to your side, protect you, and take you home. The psalmist had that confidence in his protector, even in the midst of his greatest pain: "In the day of my trouble I will call to you, for you will answer me" (Ps. 86:7). He knew that he had a Savior who was listening.

So do you.

THE POINT OF HEALING

It took months for Brian's frustration to well up to the point of anger. When it broke, his journey to spiritual healing was mercifully quick.

"That day in the car, I really let my anger erupt," he says. "As Sheila and I talked, I became more and more furious until I just broke down, sobbing before God — *Why did You do this to me? Why won't You take away my pain?* I was bitter about my condition — and unforgiving toward the man who had caused the accident."

Somewhere in that storm God spoke to Brian. "He hit me in the heart," Brian says.

"In an instant, I saw myself as I really was, angry and bitter. I knew I needed to forgive the man who hurt me. I cried out to God, *Forgive me, Lord. I forgive the man who hurt me — please take this bitterness away from me.*"

That's when the peace came. "I can take you to the exact spot on the highway where it happened," Brian smiles. "That's the place where healing began for me."

Later, Brian learned that grace had been at work in his life in ways he never knew. The doctors who performed surgery on him were Christians and had prayed for him before the operation.

Brian has settled into a good career as a fund-raiser for a respected parachurch ministry, but he continues to battle pain. "My healing was not physical," he admits. "I have pain every day." He suffers more than even his closest associates know. His daily regimen of four powerful medications is never quite able to control the discomfort from his damaged sciatic nerve and other nagging injuries. "I can't stand or sit for too long before the pain becomes too intense," he admits. "Nearly every day I close my office door and break into tears from the pain."

But he has rediscovered the faith that

believes God not for what we see but for what we don't see, faith that believes in spite of suffering. "I chose to be thankful for being alive instead of focusing on the pain," he says. "I thank God that I can walk and that I have a supportive family. And I pray that God will keep on giving me the grace to endure."

Brian also finds opportunities to preach from time to time, and he never passes them up. His favorite text? 2 Cor. 12:9 — "My grace is sufficient for you, for my power is made perfect in weakness."

That same grace is yours — if you will reach out to accept it.

Your Journey

Exploring Your Story

1. In what ways is your story similar to Brian's? How is it different?

2. List some of the ways pain has affected your life. First list the physical effects, then the spiritual ones.

3. What actions have you taken to manage your pain physically and spiritually?

Exploring God's Word

1. Read chapters 1 and 2 of Job. When you suffer pain, are your reactions more like Job's or more like his wife's? Why do you

think that is?

2. Job's "comforters" were really his accusers, since they tried to convince him that his suffering resulted from his own sin. Read John 9:1–3, and then write a brief answer to Job's friends.

3. Do a brief study on suffering in Rom. 8:28–29; 1 Pet. 1:3–12; and Heb. 12:1–12. Based on these scriptures, why do you think we suffer? How should we respond when we do?

Exploring the Steps to Healing

1. Of the steps to healing listed in this chapter, which have you already taken, and which have you yet to take?

2. When you feel angry, what or whom are you angry about? What have you done to process your anger? Is there more that you can or should do?

3. Interview someone who suffers from a chronic illness yet seems to remain hopeful and cheerful. Ask him or her, "What's your secret?"

7
REGRET

FROM GUILT TO PARDON

Point of Healing
I can leave my past behind
because God has forgiven me.

His blood can make the foulest clean;
His blood avails for me.
— Charles Wesley

"It's 50 bucks a night plus tips," the manager said flatly, blowing smoke into Renee's face. "How old are you, kid?"

"Eighteen," she replied, lying.

"You ever dance before?"

Orange and blue spotlights played on the walls of the dimly lit Atlanta nightclub. Renee LeClair glanced at the woman on the elevated stage, nearly naked, gyrating to the beat of seductive music. The desperate 17-year-old thought briefly of Jamie, her infant son, and of her cocaine-addicted boyfriend

157

who had ordered her to "go get some money — or else."

"Sure," she said, lying again. "I'll be back at eight o'clock."

"I had come to believe that was the only thing I could do," Renee recalls. "I had no education, no way to make a living. I couldn't even fill out an application for a decent job."

Before long, dancing at strip clubs became a way of life. "I was beyond shame," she admits. "I had such low self-esteem that I actually needed the applause and whistles of the men who lined the stage. I felt that worthless."

Sexually molested as a child, Renee's opinion of herself was shaded by that experience. Yet without realizing it, she began a pattern of behavior that led her deeper and deeper into misery. As a teenager, she felt that she was unattractive and unintelligent. But she discovered one way of making herself attractive. "Sex was my only asset," she recalls bitterly. "It was the one thing I could use to make people respond to me."

Renee's lifestyle — dancing every evening, living with a man who abused her verbally and physically — soon took the inevitable toll on her spirit. "I wasn't whole," she admits. "I didn't even know myself. But when I took off my clothes and danced, people cheered for me."

The payment for that nightly affirmation was despair. Alcohol and drugs became her one release. "I needed the drug high to cover up what I felt like inside," she remembers. "I couldn't deal with me."

Renee's relationship with her boyfriend typified her miserable existence. Five years older than she, he had seemed like a savior at first. Within days after she moved into his seedy apartment, their relationship turned violent. "I needed someone to love me," Renee recalls, "but I settled for someone who would supply my cocaine habit."

When her abusive boyfriend left, Renee was devastated. "He left me for another dancer at the club," she says. "I was even more humiliated. I felt so alone. I guess that was why I was so attracted to Tyler."

Tyler was the son of a prominent Savannah clergyman and was living something of a prodigal's life. He was rebelling against his parents' influence and against God. "When he walked into the club and offered to buy me a drink, I knew that if I accepted, I wouldn't be alone anymore."

They soon married, and together they lived a stormy, abusive relationship that took them lower than either had been before.

"I didn't stop drinking," Renee remembers, "even during my pregnancy with Jessica. I was taking drugs to get high and drinking alcohol to come down."

"And I was completely out of control," Tyler adds. "One night we both got pretty drunk and began to fight. I put a knife to her throat. I almost killed her."

Renee's drug addiction escalated, and her behavior grew more and more erratic. "I was a very angry person," she said. "I was emotionally destroyed on the inside. When I wasn't high, I was sad. And so nervous — I just couldn't focus on anything. Getting high was the only thing I lived for."

At two o'clock one Sunday morning, flashing lights appeared in her rearview mirror. Fifteen minutes later, Renee failed a field sobriety test. It was her third arrest for driving while intoxicated. She knew that she would serve time in jail.

As Renee sat in the back of the police cruiser, her hands cuffed behind her back, she thought of the five years since she had left home. She tried to remember a time when she wasn't addicted to cocaine, a time when she didn't have to humiliate herself onstage every night. She wondered if Tyler really loved her, if he would help her now.

And she thought of Jamie, now four years old, and Jessica, not quite two. "My babies," she whispered. "Who's gonna take care of my babies?"

The cruiser pulled away from the curb, red lights still flashing. Renee laid her head against the window and began to cry.

THE EFFECT OF REGRET

It's been going on for a long time. Ever since there have been people, there's been sin. It's something about the way we're wired. We ought to do what's right, and we know it. But we don't. Every human being has that same selfish streak. We'll do what we want, and it's just too bad for anybody who tries to stop us.

That's called sin.

Brazilian rock star Cassia Eller was known for her unconventional lifestyle, one that mocked the morals of her home country. She said, "There is no such thing as right or wrong. You choose what's good for you, and it ends up working out well."[1] Of course, we know that it doesn't always work out so well. Guilt and grief eventually make their way into the heart of the spiritual rebel. The havoc that results from their presence has been cataloged throughout history. Since the creation of the world, sin has brought the same set of consequences to just about everybody. We sin in big ways and in small ones, but the results are always the same: We're alienated from God, from others, and from ourselves. As Renee put it, we aren't whole.

Here's a laundry list of the effect of past sin. Some of it may sound familiar.

Guilt

Nobody has to tell you that you've done something wrong. You just know. Sure, you can deny it. "Who, me?" But deep inside, you know something's not right.

Renee knew. As much as she needed the whistles and cheers of the club patrons, she knew there was something wrong about it.

Guilt is that crummy feeling you get when you blow up at the kids. *I shouldn't have done that.* Guilt is that nagging voice in the back of your mind. *You can't keep doing this. It's wrong, you know.* Guilt is often at the root of problems with self-esteem. *I hate myself for what I've done.*

Humorist Erma Bombeck referred to guilt as the gift that keeps on giving. When you do wrong, it camps in your heart and just won't go away.

Shame

An ad in the January 26, 2003, edition of the *Corpus Christi Caller-Times* gave new meaning to the expression "Come clean." Regino Salinas took out a full page to confess that he had run a red light while talking on his cell phone and caused an accident that killed two people.[2] Not everyone is so forthright with failure, however. Our tendency is to hide what we've done.

Three-year-olds hide. They hide from their mommies when they've broken a rule. Criminals hide. They hide what they do and the evidence of what they've done. Addicts hide. They hide their addiction. They hide their behavior. They're ashamed of what they've done.

And they're not alone. At one time or another, all of us have pulled the shawl of guilt over our eyes and have hidden some action or attitude that caused pain. We hide our behavior from others. We hide it from God, or we try to. Most of all, we hide it from ourselves. *At least I'm not as bad as her. I can quit this. Anytime. I know I can. Problem? I don't have a problem. You've got the problem.*

We hide because we're ashamed — and we're not alone. Adam and Eve were the first to sin, the first to feel shame, and the

163

first to hide (see Gen. 3:8–10).

Alienation from God

"Go."

With that word, God banished the first human pair from the Garden of Eden and from His presence. The inevitable result of our sin, of our rebellion against God, is that we forfeit a relationship with Him. When we live our lives selfishly, we're at odds with God. The result, as theologian Paul Tillich observed, is that there is within every person a "God-shaped hole."

When you live your life estranged from God, there's something wrong that you can't quite put your finger on. The feeling exhibits itself in many different ways. We feel low self-esteem. We're restless. We wonder about the purpose of life. We love it but seem at odds with it at the same time. Life seems incomplete.

We don't need something else — more money, a bigger home, a new car, a better job. We need some*one*. We were made for a relationship with God, and we don't feel whole without it.

Alienation from Others

God isn't the only one who grieves over self-ish behavior. Girlfriends, husbands, coworkers, and friends also tire of dealing with someone whose life is centered on himself or herself. The consequences of sin on human relationships are devastating. Ruined relationships, lost jobs, broken trust, hurt feelings, bitterness, estrangement: these are the fruit of sin. Rudyard Kipling wrote, "The sin they do by two and two they must pay for one by one." The utter loneliness of sin's consequence is devastating but true.

Chris Campbell's star had risen quickly in the publishing business. His start-up company produced training manuals for some of the largest corporations in his major metropolitan city. Within five years, there wasn't a publisher in the area that could match his print orders. Chris soon expanded the business regionally. He had success and the trappings that go with it: a home in a gated community, luxury cars, membership in the city club. Some of the most influential men and women of his city became his closest friends.

But Chris's ambition was not satisfied; he wanted more. He started another, riskier venture and persuaded influential friends to invest. The venture soon foundered, but rather than admit the losses, Chris devised a scheme. He began using new investors' checks to pay off existing clients, never admitting that the venture had failed. Within months, Chris was buried in financial promises — and debt. The new business toppled first, and other things soon followed. The publishing business, his home, his cars, and finally his reputation were gone.

At Chris's trial, the broken man tried to explain himself. "I just can't believe I did this. I never intended to hurt anyone." That weak excuse sounded no better to his friends than it did to the judge. His influential contacts deserted him. He now wears his shame in the same uncomfortable way he wears his prison uniform.

Despair

Sin, like many things, becomes a habit in time. More accurately, sin *is* a habit, an inbred trait that manifests itself consistently in our lives. We rebel against it at times, but the current is strong. Eventually, some come to believe that sin is inevitable, change impossible.

The apostle Paul described that feeling perfectly:

> I do not understand what I do. For what I want to do I do not do, but what I hate I do. And if I do what I do not want to do, I

agree that the law is good. As it is, it is no longer I myself who do it, but it is sin living in me. I know that nothing good lives in me, that is, in my sinful nature. For I have the desire to do what is good, but I cannot carry it out. For what I do is not the good I want to do; no, the evil I do not want to do — this I keep on doing. Now if I do what I do not want to do, it is no longer I who do it, but it is sin living in me that does it. So I find this law at work: When I want to do good, evil is right there with me. For in my inner being I delight in God's law; but I see another law at work in the members of my body, waging war against the law of my mind and making me a prisoner of the law of sin at work within my members. What a wretched man I am! Who will rescue me from this body of death? *(Rom. 7:15–24).*

In time, it becomes easy to conclude, as Renee did, that no change is possible. The selfish life is a life of despair. Unhappy with the way we are, we feel powerless to change. Like Paul, we wonder, *Who can get me out of this mess?* There is an answer. God's Word points the way.

Jesus was a master storyteller. Seated on the windswept hillsides of Galilee, reclining in the firelit homes of friends in Bethany, teaching in the Temple court, walking along the road, Jesus taught His followers by using parables — engaging stories that made a spiritual point. His masterpiece, His signature story, the most touching and perhaps most meaningful of all Jesus' parables, is the story of a young man who followed the path of desire to its bitter end. It's a story of sin. More than that, it's a story of redemption. Weaving a tale of sorrow and disappointment, Jesus used the all-too-believable story of one young man's tragic failure to illustrate the grandest theme in Scripture: No matter who you are, no matter what you have done, God loves you, and He wants you back. The story is recorded in Luke 15.

Selfish Choices

There was a man, said Jesus, who had two sons. The older son was steady, reliable, never a worry to his parents. The younger son, as younger sons often are, was full of life and anxious to live it. Jesus gave the lad no name, but for centuries he has been known as the prodigal son. "Prodigal" means wasteful or extravagant, and the young man was. When he was barely of legal age he left home to see the world. He was not interested in education; he had no desire to enter business. He wanted to live, to experience life and everything in it.

He did exactly that.

Faraway places always seem more exciting, so he went far from home. Money attracts friends instantly, and he had many. Alcohol enlivens any gathering, so he threw wild parties. Women are always available to rich young men, and they were available to him. Like the rich bachelor on a reality television show, he had his choice of pretty girls. He could give them a rose of acceptance, and they would be unaware of the accompanying thorn — the fact that his money was quickly slipping away.

Finally free from the constraints of home, family, and responsibility, the prodigal son acted upon every desire that he felt. He was selfish, wasteful, and self-indulgent. This young man cared nothing for his father's wishes, instead wasting his time and money on every vain impulse that entered his head. In the same way, we sin when, caring nothing for God's wishes and ignoring His guidance, we choose to go our own way, behaving in whatever manner we judge will be most gratifying. Flaunting our insolence, like the true-life thief who wore to his court appearance the shoes he stole from the mall, we act as if our behavior has no consequences.

Meanwhile, back at home, the young man's father rose each day, and before setting about the business of the day, he would cast a longing look toward the horizon. *Maybe today I'll see him. Maybe today my son will come home.* The anxious pacing became routine, revealing as much about the love of the father as about the licentious nature of the son. In the same way, God is always eager for our return, no matter where we've been, no matter what we've done.

Inevitable Consequences

One day the party ended, as parties must. The money ran out, the wine stopped flowing, the women grew bored, the friends moved on. Just as quickly as they had begun, the good times were over. The young man found himself penniless, alone, and far from home. Like a sailor on a small craft caught in a squall, he soon realized that he was in real trouble. Desperate for food, he took a job at a nearby farm, feeding garbage to the hogs. *I'm so hungry,* he thought. *I wonder if anyone would notice if I took some for myself.* His "champagne wishes and caviar dreams" became a nightmare of rotting scraps fit for hogs.

Selfish behavior brings a matched set of consequences: brokenness and shame. The results are no different for us. As Renee put it, we can't stand ourselves, but we don't know how to change.

The Turning Point

Finally the young man came to his senses. *This is nuts,* he thought. *If I go home, I'll be a laughingstock, but at least I'll have something to eat.* Resolving to face whatever consequences lay before him, he started out on the long journey home. Packing his few belongings, he made his way back to the place where he knew he really belonged.

Every lost soul must make that same decision — the decision to go home. That turning point comes when we decide that life with God is better than life without Him. That can't happen until we're honest with ourselves about the mess we're in. It's the moment when we say to ourselves and to God, *I blew it. I've messed up my life, and I know it's my fault. I need Your help.*

Without a turning point there can be no change. Until we turn from rebellion, there will be no joy-filled homecoming. In order to be reconciled with God, one must be sorry for sin — sorry enough to quit.

Free Forgiveness

But the harsh reaction the boy had expected never materialized. While he was still a long way off, his father — pacing and looking down the road as usual — saw him coming. He ran to meet him, and they stood there, face-to-face, beside the road. Grief and shame, guilt and loneliness fell at the feet of forgiveness.

"Father," the boy stammered. "I'm not worthy to be your son . . . I . . . I'll work as one of the servants if you'll just let me come home."

The father listened to the boy's conditions, but he swept them away. Immediately, strong arms embraced the boy, "My son," he declared with his prophetic word. "My son was lost, and now he's found." The sentence fell onto a shivering heart like a warm blanket.

The father raved on: "My son was dead, and now he's alive again!" The pronouncement made perfect sense to the boy. For so long he had felt so empty — so dead. Now, he felt alive again.

There was a party that night like nothing you've ever seen. Feasting, dancing, lots of music. All the neighbors were invited. The old man dressed the boy up in his best suit and paraded him around like an astronaut who had just returned from the moon. Everybody who walked in the door got the same speech. "This is my boy. I'm so proud of him. I'm so glad he came home."

That's the way God is. No matter where you've been, no matter what you've done, no matter how far you've gone, no matter how long you've stayed away, He's always ready to welcome you home. In His heart, He's been pacing, casting lingering looks in your direction. All this time there's been an empty place at His table, an empty coat hook by the door, an unopened present under the tree. There's a missing place in God's family, the place where you're supposed to be.

For thousands of years God has been welcoming prodigals home. One by one, He has extended His embrace to every returning prodigal. But there's one reunion yet to take place, one celebration yet to be held, one weary soul yet to embrace.

You.

STEPS TO HEALING

There's nothing complicated about grace; it's the simplest idea in the world. We're all rotten sinners before we come to Him in repentance, but God loves us anyway. Even though we've ignored Him, disobeyed Him, run from Him, hidden from Him, or even cursed Him, He's always willing to forgive, always eager to bring us back into fellowship with Him.

And that grace is remarkably easy to receive. The process begins for you in the same place it did for the prodigal son in Jesus' story — the place where you come to the end of yourself and admit that you must change.

Confess Your Sin

"I was wrong." They're tiny little words, but they're difficult to say — so difficult, in fact, that many people never say them. To be rid of sin, we must own it: we must admit that we're guilty. That's confession.

Are you willing to take a hard look at yourself? Are you ready to admit the troubling truth that somewhere in the back of your mind you've always known? The road to healing begins with a simple choice, the decision to acknowledge what God and everybody else already knows: you have sinned.

Accept God's Gift of Forgiveness

Forgiveness is a gift, but not everybody wants it. Many people, in fact, would rather work for it than receive it free, for nothing. It's humbling to be forgiven. We live by the bootstrap. *I can do this. If I broke it, I'll fix it. Sure, I was wrong, but I'll make it up to you. Put it on my card.*

The only problem with that is that it's impossible. Sin is the one problem you can't fix on your own. There's no way to turn back the clock on selfish behavior. Every one of us has broken things that we're helpless to repair.

That's why forgiveness is called a gift. God forgives us not because we deserve it, not because we've earned it, but precisely because we can't. What we can't do for ourselves He does for us.

Are you willing to humble yourself and admit that you need God's help to fix your life?

Resolve to Live a New Life

What God wants for all of us, of course, is for our hearts to change. Sure, you can ask for God's forgiveness, receive it, and then go right back and live the same life as before. And if you come back sometime later and ask forgiveness again, He'll give it.

God doesn't hold a grudge. Unlike your boss or your kids or your spouse, He'll forgive you as often as you ask.

But is that any way to live, stuck in a cycle of guilt and failure?

God wants something better for you. Jesus called it the abundant life (John 10:10). The apostle Paul asks the obvious question "What shall we say, then? Shall we go on sinning so that grace may increase? By no means!" (Rom. 6:1–2). Later he describes the change that should take place in each of our lives. "Do not conform any longer to the pattern of this world, but be transformed by the renewing of your mind. Then you will be able to test and approve what God's will is — his good, pleasing and perfect will" (Rom. 12:2). When you accept God's forgiveness, you must determine to live a new life — to be a changed person.

And with His help, you can be changed.

Make Things Right with Others

There's one more thing. Once we've been reconciled to God, it makes sense that we should be reconciled with others.

Sinful behavior hurts. It hurts us. It hurts our relationship with God. And it hurts others too. Spouses are injured by our hurtful words and actions. Employers are cheated when we rob them of time or possessions. Boyfriends, girlfriends, in-laws, neighbors, coworkers — the list goes on.

There's a word for "making things right" between yourself and someone else. It's called *restitution.* It's packing up your belongings and taking the long trek back to the house of forgiveness. If there's someone you've harmed, apologize. And offer to do what you can to make it right.

THE POINT OF HEALING

A surgeon uses a knife as an instrument of healing. In the same way, God may use pain to begin spiritual healing. Renee's healing began with incarceration.

"When I was in jail, someone gave me a Bible," she reports. "I never had a Bible of my own. I started reading it every night until lights out." One day, in a rare moment of privacy, Renee read 2 Cor. 6:2 — " 'In the time of my favor I heard you, and in the day of salvation I helped you.' I tell you, now is the time of God's favor, now is the day of salvation."

"At that moment, the Lord spoke to me. He said, *It's time, Renee.*"

Meanwhile at home, Tyler was exhausted from working all day, picking up the kids from the baby-sitter, and watching them all night. "I missed Renee, but I didn't miss the constant fighting."

Five months later, Renee, clean and sober, was freed through a work-release program. A few weeks after that, Tyler made an unusual request. "Let's go to church this Sunday. It's Easter, and Mom and Dad invited us to go to their church and have dinner with them."

It's time, Renee.

"I don't have good-enough clothes to go to your dad's church," Renee argued. "I'll feel so out of place among all those Christians. We'll have to go all the way to Savannah." Renee raised every objection she could think of, but in the end, the still, small voice was more persuasive. It was time.

The upbeat worship service provided a stark contrast to the darkness of Renee's soul. "It seemed like every song had the word *alive* in it," she remembers. "I kept thinking, *I wish I was alive.*"

For Tyler, the service was a simple reminder of long-forgotten truth. *I'm home,* he thought. *This is where I belong.*

The pastor's message touched a corner of Renee and Tyler's hearts they thought they had closed off. When the invitation to step forward and receive Christ was given, they both knew: *It's time.*

"Tyler took me by the hand, looked into my eyes, and then gave a slight motion with his head toward the front," Renee says. "I didn't hesitate. I gave my past to God that day — and He gave me a future."

Their hearts changed in an instant, but much of their lives remained a struggle. When Renee quit her dancing job, their income was cut in half. Financial stress combined with the challenge of being a blended family threatened to sidetrack their new life. "It seemed like Satan used those family struggles to tear away at our faith," Tyler says. But the couple persevered. With help from their new church family in Atlanta, they held on to their newfound faith and each other. Renee began taking courses at a community college and now has a job as a medical secretary. "Now we have a home, not just a house," she says, beaming. "God took our broken lives, all the things that we'd messed up, and turned them into something beautiful."

He'll do it for you.

Few people's lives are as dramatically self-destructive as Renee and Tyler's. Yet every person has sinned, and every one of us has suffered the effects of sin. What sin has destroyed, God can reclaim. The journey to healing begins with confession. *Lord, I've failed You. I've failed others. I've failed myself. I was wrong, and I'm sorry.*

Are you ready to make the journey from brokenness to new life?

It's time.

Your Journey

Exploring Your Story

1. In what ways is your story like Renee's? How is it different?

2. In what ways has your past behavior — your sin — affected your relationships with others?

3. Describe the effects of guilt on your life? When have you been most aware of it? How does it feel?

Exploring God's Word

1. Read Luke 15:11–32. What do you think motivated the younger son to leave home and behave as he did? Why does this pattern of behavior (though often less dramatic) occur so often in human beings?

2. List some words that describe the father's attitude toward his sons.

3. Since this story is really about us and our relationships to God, write a brief paragraph that describes how God feels

about us and how we can be reunited to Him.

Exploring the Steps to Healing

1. Have you ever made a full confession of your sin to God? Have you ever made a full confession to the people you have most offended?

2. The prodigal son made the choice to return to his father, even though it was humiliating to do so. What will it take for you to be willing to "go home," that is, to turn to God and seek reconciliation with Him?

3. List the names of those you have offended by your behavior. Spend some time in prayer, asking God to give you guidance as to when and how to seek reconciliation with them.

8

Disability

FROM FRUSTRATION TO PURPOSE

Point of Healing
I accept myself just as I am
because I know that my life has meaning.

No pain, no palm; no thorns, no throne;
no gall, no glory; no cross, no crown.
— William Penn

"Are your parents here?"

The question took Don Hernandez by surprise. Physical exams for summer camp were a matter of routine. He'd had one every year for the past three, and there was nothing to it except for the booster shot — nobody likes needles. *What's this about?* he wondered.

Miguel and Inez Hernandez stood next to their son, who was seated on the examining table. The doctor closed the door and leaned against it. "It's diabetes," he said

182

emphatically. "Your son has juvenile onset diabetes, Type 1. He'll need insulin injections for the rest of his life."

Shots, Don thought. *I hate shots — but at least I'll live a normal life.*

"And there's more," the doctor said. "His blood sugar level is above 400 right now. Don's not going to summer camp. He's going to the hospital for immediate treatment."

"That was the day my life changed forever," Don recalls. "Every dream I'd ever had went out the window in five minutes — and I didn't even know it."

Over the next 47 years Don would struggle against his disease. Fighting every day to be normal, he waged war with his own body, trying to keep his blood sugar level under control. Too much food, and he could lapse into diabetic coma; too little, and insulin shock might result. "Every day was a battle," Don reflects. "And I often lost. No matter how carefully I managed my diet or how regularly I tested my blood sugar, I just couldn't keep it level — I couldn't live a normal life."

Few milestones are as important in the life of a young person as earning a driver's license. "I was so proud of that thing," Don recalls. "I loved the freedom. For the first time in my life I could go where I wanted to go." And he did, until diabetes affected his eyesight. "I couldn't see well enough to drive, and I knew it," he recalls. "I surrendered my driver's license. At that point, I was fighting just to keep my eyesight."

Don's frustration intensified over the next few years as he was continually forced to accommodate himself to his disease. Eating regular meals was imperative, so travel was difficult. When the senior class went to London, Don went to the mall. College life, with its late-night pizza parties and irregular sleep patterns, was impossible for Don. He dropped out, got a job, and eventually enrolled in a community college.

Sports were another interest. "I figured I could live without a car if I could still play basketball," Don says. "I loved the game; I was pretty good at it too. But I was unable to continue." Diabetes attacked Don's extremities, forming sores on his feet. "When I had to have toes removed, I went from being frustrated to being mad," Don said. "My disease had become a prison. I was trapped in my own body."

Over the next several years Don continued to rage against his disease, finally gaining some ground. Grabbing life with desperate determination, he pursued his greatest ambition — to enter the ministry. When his eyesight improved, he renewed his driver's license. He fell in love with Sharon Gonzales, and the two were married. Soon afterward, he became a volunteer youth pastor at a church in San Antonio.

After 10 years of part-time schoolwork, Don completed his education and accepted a ministry position at another church in Texas. For several years his life and ministry went along without a hitch — except for the occasional diabetic crisis, like the time he slipped into a coma while driving home from church. "I almost made it," he deadpans. "And I would have, too, if it hadn't been for that fire hydrant on State Street." Having lost consciousness, Don ran over the hydrant, sending a geyser of water high into the air. "I missed the whole show," he jokes. What he didn't miss was the $1,200 repair bill from the city.

Don continued to manage his diabetes with insulin injections. He and Sharon moved to a church in Phoenix where he became children's pastor and developed a clown character, complete with silly costumes and a suitcase full of props.

Oddly, one effect of diabetes became a blessing in disguise. When Don's kidneys failed, he was convinced that his ministry, perhaps even his life, was over. But a rare opportunity for a kidney and pancreas transplant came his way. Following the transplant surgery, Don gradually gained new strength. The new pancreas began to maintain his blood sugar level, so he was able to discontinue insulin injections. Life became tolerable, if not exactly normal. *I'm actually going to make it,* Don thought. *I'm going to beat this disease. After all these years of fighting, I'm finally going to have a normal life.*

What Don couldn't overcome was the long-term effect of diabetes on his body. Poor circulation, a common condition among diabetics, caused sores on his feet and lower legs. The sores refused to heal and eventually became open wounds. Every day the pain grew worse until he was finally hospitalized.

On a Thursday afternoon, Don sat on the edge of the hospital bed, waiting for the doctor to arrive. He recalled the years of battling diabetes, and he prayed, *Not my leg, God. I can't lose my leg. I've covered up for You all these years. I've fought against this disease all these years and never complained. I've ministered for You; I've preached Your Word. I've lived in this body like a prison cell.*

Please, Lord, give me this one thing. Give me my leg.

The doctor entered the room, closed the door, and leaned against it. "The treatment isn't working, Don. Your leg must come off."

"No."

"There's no choice, Don. We've tried every other option."

"I said *no.*"

"All right. This has to be your decision, but you need to know that it's your leg or your life. If you insist on keeping your leg, you will die. I'll give you a day to think it over."

The door swung shut, and the doctor's steps echoed down the hallway. Don sat alone in the hospital room. He remembered the 13-year-old boy sitting in the infirmary at summer camp. He remembered the driver's license and the basketball court and the trip to London he never took. He remembered the endless blood tests and the needles and the comas and the surgeries. "All I ever wanted was a normal life," he said.

The Effect of Disability

Disability locks a healthy person into an imperfect body. Disability seeps from the body into the soul, salting the well of joy.

Disabled is an unpopular term these days but very accurate. Whether due to illness or injury, scores of people are not able to function as they wish. A study commissioned by the National Institute on Disability and Rehabilitation Research estimates that 37.7 million people in the United States, some 15 percent, suffer from some limitation of activity. Of those, 11.5 million are unable to perform their major activity.[1] Paraplegics are not the only disabled. Those who suffer from arthritis, diabetes, heart disease, or a host of other common ailments may appear healthy but suffer limitations because of their disease. There are some things they cannot do, and other things — treatments, therapies — that they must do in order to survive. Their lives are governed not by their own will but by the weakness of their bodies.

Frustration

The disabled are prevented from doing things that most of us take for granted or even find annoying. A disabled person may be unable to wash the car, mow the lawn, or take the dog for a walk. He or she may be unable to travel, unable to read, unable to enjoy intimacy with a spouse. Those limitations cause frustration. *Why can't I be normal — like everyone else? You guys go ahead. I'll just stay home this time. What I wouldn't give to be able to rake the yard!*

Fear
Disability forces one to confront the reality that healthy people ignore: our bodies are wearing out. Disabled people know it because they deal with it every day. That knowledge inevitably brings fear about the future: *What's going to happen to my body next? How will I make a living? How can I provide for my family if I can't even take care of myself? Who will take care of me?*

Disillusionment
One by one, a disabled person lists the things that have been lost. They begin to add up:

- I'll never climb a mountain.

- I'll never have children.

- I'll never go to Europe.

- I'll never drive a car again.

Disillusionment may be occasional or constant. Either way, life comes to be

189

defined by what is *not* possible rather than by what is.

Anger

Sooner or later, frustration boils into anger. The negligent doctor. The careless driver. The disease. The world. There may be many objects of the anger, but one in particular underlies them all — God. *Life isn't fair. I shouldn't have to live this way. Why did this happen to me?*

God is the object of each accusation. It is God with whom we wrestle in our hearts. We know that He's responsible for the entire world — and for us. The question springs almost automatically from an honest heart: *Why me?* Even the greatest heroes of faith had their moments of doubt. David asked, "Has God forgotten to be merciful? Has he in anger withheld his compassion?" (Ps. 77:9). It was as if David were saying, *Excuse me, Lord — did You forget that I'm on Your team?*

Anger may also produce resentment toward those who enjoy good health. That resentment can take the form of manipulation, or it may be purely internal, poisoning the heart of the disabled person.

Self-pity

Those who are unable to function as they once did suffer a loss of self-esteem. Their pride in themselves, once a portrait of strength and agility, is now a faded canvas of weakness and limitation. They may look in the mirror in a new way, perceiving themselves as objects of pity rather than whole persons. *Nobody could fall in love with me. What good am I? The best days of my life are gone.*

Disability is often permanent. For a disabled person, dreams of perfect health may be unrealistic. *Normal* has a new definition, one that includes some loss of function. For them, the question is how to deal with life on these new terms.

One of the apostles suffered a chronic physical problem. In spite of that, he became the first missionary in Europe, organized dozens of churches, wrote half of the books in the New Testament, and kept a remarkably peaceful attitude about his chronic problem.

His name was Paul.

GOD'S WORD

A former persecutor of Christians, the apostle Paul was the most successful missionary of the Early Church, taking the Good News throughout Asia Minor and Greece, planting churches and appointing elders as he went.

But success had a price. Paul faced opposition from nonbelievers whose way of life was threatened by the Good News and from believers who challenged his authority as an apostle spreading false teaching among new Christians. As he stayed on the road constantly, preaching nearly every day, supporting himself with his trade as a tentmaker, facing opposition from outsiders and even fellow Christians, the last thing he needed was a disability. But that's what he got. He discusses this infirmity in one of his letters, referring to it as a "thorn in the flesh."

Scholars disagree over what Paul's "thorn" actually was. Some argue that "thorn in the flesh" was simply Paul's way of describing the constant conflict he endured with certain groups of Christians. Most, however, believe that this thorn was some illness or condition that produced a form of chronic illness or disability. Epilepsy and stuttering have often been suggested as possibilities. So in addition to leading the church during a very tumultuous period of history, Paul had to cope with the limitations of his own body. That gives him something in common with those of us who live in a body that's weaker than our will.

Characteristic of the great apostle, he thought clearly about the implications of his condition. He understood both why he suffered it and how to cope with it. We can learn much from his few insightful words on the subject:

> To keep me from becoming conceited because of these surpassingly great revelations, there was given me a thorn in my flesh, a messenger of Satan, to torment me. Three times I pleaded with the Lord to take it away from me. But he said to me, "My grace is sufficient for you, for my power is made perfect in weakness." Therefore I will boast all the more gladly about my weaknesses, so that Christ's power may rest on me. That is why, for Christ's sake, I delight in weaknesses, in insults, in hardships, in persecutions, in difficulties. For when I am weak, then I am strong *(2 Cor. 12:7–10)*.

God Does Not Cause Disability but Rather Allows It

Paul refers to his condition as a "messenger of Satan" (v. 7). That interesting turn of phrase reveals an essential truth: God does not cause illness but rather allows it.

Our tendency to blame God for our condition acknowledges that we believe God is fully in control of the world. After all, if God isn't behind what happens to us, who is? Paul lays the blame for evil in the right place — with Satan. It's not God but Satan who actively inflicts illness, disease, and disability on human beings.

Yet Paul rightly acknowledges that God *allows* evil — of which disability is one form. The distinction is not mere hairsplitting. Satan desires only our complete destruction. Everything he does is aimed at our eventual ruin. God desires only our good. It's true that He allows evil to exist and allows Satan to inflict it upon us at times. Job is the most famous example of this (see Job 1:12; 2:6). God's purpose, however, is always redemptive. He wants to bring about some good result in our lives. That was true for Paul, and it's true for you.

Your Life Has Purpose

Paul identified the good result that would come from his suffering. He realized that as an apostle he was given a great privilege and was even allowed to see visions of heaven. He was a great leader in the

Church. One possible result of spiritual authority is spiritual pride. Those who are given great privileges sometimes believe that they're extraordinary people. Perhaps Paul saw this tendency in himself. He believed that the reason he suffered this thorn in the flesh was to keep him from becoming conceited. Disability is always humbling.

Yet it would be wrong to assume that God allows disability in your life simply to take you down a peg. Like Paul, you may need that occasionally, but that's not the only reason God allows people to suffer illness or disability.

It may be difficult to discern the reason that you suffer. In fact, it may be impossible to identify it. Unlike Paul's situation, God's motive for allowing your disability may not be at all clear-cut. Some well-meaning people may try to offer facile reasons for your suffering: "God picked you because you're special." Some may even offer judgmental opinions: "Maybe God's trying to teach you not to drive so fast." Reject all such nonsensical advice, no matter how well intended it may be.

In the end, comfort comes from knowing that God is in control. It's we who feel the need to have all things explained. God is often content to allow our questions to go unanswered. Yet as the Bible promises, His plans are always perfect. " 'I know the plans I have for you,' declares the LORD, 'plans to prosper you and not to harm you, plans to give you hope and a future' " (Jer. 29:11).

Your life does have a purpose, even if you're not able to function as others do.

God's Grace Is Good Enough

Paul didn't enjoy being disabled any more than we do. He hated it. Three times he begged God to take this thorn in the flesh away from him. Every disabled person knows the depth of those prayers.

God chose not to remove Paul's thorn, though. Instead, He left Paul with this promise: "My grace is sufficient for you." In other words, God said to Paul, "I won't take away your problem, but I'll help you manage it."

God's grace is good enough. It's good enough to provide the mental and physical courage you need to cope with a body that doesn't work. It's good enough to provide the income, care, and support you need. It's good enough to make your life productive, even if some part of your body doesn't function as it should.

God's promise to you is the same as it was to Paul: *You can make it. I'll help.*

Weakness Is Greater than Strength

By suffering some limitation, Paul discovered one of the most profound and paradoxical truths in Scripture: weakness is greater than strength. Jesus embodied that truth when He "made himself nothing" (Phil. 2:7), leaving His position of authority in heaven to be born as a human being. He demonstrated it dramatically by His death and resurrection, proving that self-sacrifice is a greater power than that wielded by any king or army.

We mistakenly believe that those with perfect bodies, good looks, or great strength are the most useful people. In fact, God delights in working through the smallest and weakest people. Og Mandino said, "Each struggle, each defeat, sharpens your skills and strengths, your courage and your endurance, your ability and your confidence and thus each obstacle is a comrade-in-arms forcing you to become better."[2]

Paul realized that if he had been perfect in every way, other people might idolize him, considering him even more important than Jesus, about whom he preached. The fact that Paul suffered some handicap made it all the more obvious that his achievements were the result of God's power, not his own ability. Remember that it was a small boy,

David, who defeated the giant Goliath. God often chooses to accomplish His will through the weakest person precisely to show that it's His strength, not ours, that counts.

The "weak" things in life really are greater than those that seem strong. Mercy is greater than vengeance, love is greater than hatred, and ants move more earth than elephants do. You are of great use to God, even though you sometimes feel helpless.

Steps to Healing

Disability affects the body, but those who have lost physical function can still be spiritually invincible. Based on Paul's example, here are some steps toward recovery of function, not in the body but in the heart.

Accept Your Condition

While it's good to be optimistic, don't ignore the implications of your disability. Accept the limitations that you must live with. That doesn't mean that you're strange or that you're a weak person. It means that you understand and accept the effects of your disease.

Accepting loss of function does not mean accepting loss of ability. Many people who cannot climb mountains find a way to stand atop them. Many who cannot see books manage to read them. Accept what you cannot do, but never surrender what you can.

Work Hard

Esther Hayes was born in a time when medical options were few. Shortly after graduating from college with a degree in music, she faced surgery to correct a defect in her spinal column. The surgery was necessary, but the side effect was heartbreaking. Her doctors faced a dilemma nearly unheard of in these days of advanced medical science. The surgeon attempted to break the news gently. "Esther, here's the decision you'll have to make. You'll either spend the rest of your life in a wheelchair, or you'll spend it lying in bed. It's up to you."

The young woman, a promising and gifted pianist, had to make her awful choice within a week. A young woman of deep faith, she talked about the surgery both with her parents and with her Heavenly Father. Before they had finished their talk, Esther knew that she would live a life of purpose and victory. Given the uncertainty surrounding any surgery in those days, Esther opted against it. She would spend most of

199

the rest of her life lying flat.

Carnegie Hall would never hear her play a piano concerto. There would be no membership in the local symphony, no walk down the aisle. Many viewed her life as over.

But Esther viewed it as a life sentence — with all the emphasis on *life.* She spent most of her 83 years lying on her back or stomach. Yet five days a week, she was wheeled over to the tall spinet piano in the living room of a home she shared with her sister. There, she gave piano lessons to students who collectively numbered in the hundreds. "This is my pulpit," Esther would say, as she patted the bed. "My students not only learn how to play the piano — they learn how to live."

By the time her students graduated to the second or third lesson book, they had learned about a God who could bring meaning to every life. Esther was their living example.

Living with a disability is simply hard work. So work at it. Take your medication. Do your exercises. You understand your body's need for rest. *Disabled* doesn't mean *not responsible.* Accept your responsibility by doing all you can. You can do more than you think.

Trust God

All people fear becoming helpless. If you have a disability, you may be more acutely aware of that possibility. You may be helpless now. That may be an advantage, because you already know that your whole life depends on God. You need Him every day, and you know it.

God has promised grace and will give you strength when you need it. He will help you cope with frustration and disappointment and enable you to face troubling situations. Are any of us truly helpless when God is on our side?

God has promised to help you. Take Him at His word.

Love Yourself

Everyone who suffers a limitation hates that limit. When your body is the limitation, it's easy — and somewhat natural — to hate yourself. Disabled people are often self-conscious or embarrassed about their bodies or their lack of ability.

Remember that God took the form of a weak, helpless baby at the birth of Christ. He suffered a humiliating and painful death on the Cross. He knows the reason for what you suffer, and He's even now accomplishing His will through you. Without saying that you love your disability, you can embrace it as God's instrument in your life and in the lives of others.

THE POINT OF HEALING

Don lay silently in bed Thursday night, but his mind was active, wrestling Jacob-like with God. He recalls a conversation that was more like a tug-of-war. "You can't take my leg, Lord. Children will be afraid of me. I won't be able to minister to them."

Don, you can minister to children without your leg. Are you sure you can minister with it?

"What are You talking about, Lord? I've given my life for You."

No, Don. You haven't. You think you're too big to be used by Me. You've been hiding your wounds, always pretending to others that you aren't sick, as if they would think less of you — or of Me. You don't have to protect Me, Don. I can use you, just as you are, just as you will be without your leg.

Just before dawn, Don reached the point of acceptance. "Lord, I'll let my wounds show," he prayed. "I'll let You have me, just as I am."

The doctor made rounds early, arriving at Don's room before 7 A.M. "What's your decision?" he asked.

"I've decided to let you amputate my leg," Don replied. It was the first time he had said the word *amputate* aloud. It wouldn't be the last.

"I don't hide my weakness anymore," Don says openly. "I try to let God be glorified in every part of me, even my illness." And He is.

Don began to view his illness as a means to minister. "I figured that in my disability God could use me to reach other people with sickness and disability." He seized John 9:1–3 as his foundation. There, Jesus' disciples asked, "Rabbi, who sinned, this man or his parents, that he was born blind?" Jesus replied, "Neither this man nor his parents sinned . . . but this happened so that the work of God might be displayed in his life" (vv. 2–3).

"That's my life," Don says. "God wants to use me as a walking billboard. He wants to strengthen others through the example of my weakness."

Five years after his amputation, Don is more active in ministry than ever, even using his prosthesis to make a point now and then. When one class of sixth graders had trouble focusing on a gospel presentation, Don sent the group out of the room, blew up an inflatable alligator prop, and attached it to his prosthetic leg. As they reentered the room, Don pretended to wrestle with the alligator, which appeared to have its jaws clamped firmly on his leg. As they sat spellbound, he pressed the button that released the components of the prosthesis, and it looked as if the giant reptile had chomped his leg in two. "I shared the gospel after that," Don says gleefully, "and boy, did they listen!"

"I embraced my weakness," Don says, "and allowed God to use it. I discovered that life has limitations — we have limitations — but we serve an unlimited God."

YOUR JOURNEY

Exploring Your Story

1. How is your story similar to Don's? How is it different?

2. Which of the effects of disability listed in this chapter characterize you? Are there some that aren't listed?

3. Write the story of your illness or disability on one sheet of paper. Describe what has happened to you and how it affects your life. Share that story with someone.

Exploring God's Word

1. Read 2 Cor. 12:7–10. List some words

that describe Paul's attitude toward his disability.

2. Why do you think God sometimes delights in using small or weak people? What mission might God have in mind for you, given your disability?

3. Do a brief study of the concept of sovereignty in the Bible, listing some verses that show that God is fully in control of the world and our lives.

Exploring the Steps to Healing

1. What is your attitude toward your disability right now? How has it changed over time?

2. Of the steps to healing listed in this chapter, which have you taken so far?

3. Interview someone with a disability that's similar to your own. Ask this person to describe how he or she came to the point of peace and acceptance about it.

9
DISAPPOINTMENT
FROM SELF-PITY TO ACTION

Point of Healing
I know that God is at work in my life
even when I don't see the results.

If you lose hope, somehow you lose the
vitality that keeps life moving, you lose
that courage to be, that quality that helps
you go on in spite of it all. And so today I
still have a dream.
— Martin Luther King Jr.

The room was painted blue — blue for boys. Two baby cribs stood ready, identical dressers beside them, filled with matching sets of boys' clothing. Neatly stacked diapers lined the low white changing table. The impossible dream of becoming parents was about to come true for Dennis and Kim Hayes — twice. Within days they would become the adoptive parents of twin boys.

"It was like a fantasy," Kim recalls. "I wanted so much to have children. When Stacie came along, it all seemed too good to be true."

Stacie was an expectant teenager from Northfield, a suburb of Chicago. For months Dennis and Kim had negotiated the adoption through their lawyer in Cincinnati. There had been interviews and paperwork, background checks, and more paperwork. Finally it was arranged. Stacie chose Dennis and Kim to adopt her babies. They would pay Stacie's health care costs. Kim would be Stacie's birth coach. Dennis and Kim would become the proud parents of not one but two baby boys.

Kim talked with Stacie nearly every day on the phone, and Dennis felt fatherly pride as he wrote the checks for Stacie's expenses — even buying candy bars to satisfy her prenatal cravings. Excited about becoming a dad, Dennis scarcely noticed that the balance on his Visa card had topped $8,000. He was at work when Kim called with the breathless announcement. "Stacie's on her way to the hospital! I'm headed to the airport!"

Kim flew to Chicago while Dennis loaded his in-laws' minivan with newborn necessities and set out for the long drive. Kim arrived for the birth, supporting Stacie through much of the 10-hour labor. Coaching gave way to crying as tiny twin lungs breathed the fresh air of planet earth for the first time. Dennis arrived two days later, and the weary couple took their newborn sons, Nathan and Daniel, to an efficiency apartment, where they would spend the state-mandated waiting period before going home to Ohio. It was late in the evening when they arrived at the motel, just before midnight on December 24, Christmas Eve.

"Those days were like a honeymoon," Dennis says. "We spent four days becoming a family."

"We did everything new parents do," Kim remembers. "We fed them. We loved them. We got up in the night with them. We became their mother and father."

On the fourth day, the phone rang in the tiny apartment. Dennis took the call. His one-syllable answers aroused Kim's attention: "Oh. Can she? How? When?"

"It was the lawyer," he said slowly, blinking tears away. "Stacie changed her mind. She wants them back."

Kim's heart stopped. "No," she sputtered. "No — she can't do that." Anger and indignation rose in her voice.

"She never signed the papers," Dennis said.

"I'll fight it. I won't allow it. These are my children!"

"Honey," Dennis said gently, searching for words to soothe his wife's anger, barely able to control his own. "Honey — there's nothing we can do."

"But she was so happy for us to take them." Kim's voice wavered. "She said we would make good parents." Tears trickled from her eyes. "She can't do this. She — she promised." Dennis gathered his helpless wife into his arms, and the two of them wept aloud as Nathan and Daniel slept peacefully on the bed.

Twenty-four hours later, the Hayses arrived alone at their empty house in Cincinnati. Dennis walked quietly to the blue room and closed the door. Kim sat in the kitchen sorting a week-old pile of newspapers.

"Any mail?" Dennis asked.

"Just junk," Kim said tiredly. "And the Visa bill — another payment for nothing."

THE EFFECT OF DISAPPOINTMENT

Disappointment is a present that comes in all shapes and sizes. Sometimes it comes in the form of a diamond ring passed back across the table. "I don't think this is going to work out. The wedding's off." Sometimes it comes as a speech from an assistant coach. "I'd like to thank you all for trying out. Those of you who weren't selected . . ." Or it may come in the form of a newborn child whose disabled body puts an end to parents' dreams of graduations and wedding days.

Canadian musician Brian Doerksen is a worship leader and writer of the familiar song "Come, Now Is the Time to Worship." He's also known disappointment and at one point considered abandoning his music career. Three of his six children were diagnosed with Fragile X Syndrome, a genetic disorder causing varying degrees of mental impairment. "Some days are overwhelming," Doerksen admits. "It's hard enough to stay on top of the needs of my children who can verbalize them, let alone figure out what the needs are of those who can't. At times I wonder how I'll be able to do this for the rest of my life." While he holds on to faith, the music leader is candid about his disappointment. When he sees other parents interacting with their children, he sometimes thinks, "I wonder if they realize how blessed they are to carry on a conversation with their child; I cry inside thinking, 'I'll never have that.' "[1]

Life seems to hold no prospect for the disappointed. They can see only more of the same disenchanting results in the future. Nearly everyone has faced some serious disappointment in life. And nearly everyone carries at least one of these painful scars on his or her spirit.

Resentment

Dennis and Kim had an obvious target for their bitter feelings: the confused young woman whose ill-thought choices shattered their dreams. It's common to identify a culprit in the scenario that casts us as the victim. *My parents let me down. My boss has never liked me. The economy made me fail.*

Resentment at those who have been the instruments of our frustration may be normal, but it's dangerous. At first it helps to have someone to blame. But like an addictive drug, what at first seems soothing soon becomes crippling. Resentment brings with it a host of other ailments.

Cynicism

For some, disappointment becomes a habit. It settles into a way of looking at life that asks, "What's the point?" The question betrays an underlying skepticism about the world and its prospects. Swiss writer Max Fischer wrote, "It's precisely the disappointing stories, which have no proper ending and therefore no proper meaning, that sound true to life."

Self-pity

Cynicism gives way finally to self-pity. And self-pity is the most destructive of all negative emotions, for it is the wellspring of both anger and apathy. Self-pity is easy to identify in others but remarkably hard to see in ourselves. It is most often revealed by comments on the good fortune of others. *Sure, anybody could succeed if they got those breaks. I guess when you're rich, everything goes right. If I could have gone to college, I'd be successful too.*

Self-pity is self-crippling. It prevents any action that leads to recovery.

Withdrawal

Stan Toler wrote, "We are spiritually and emotionally vulnerable when we face changes in the routine of our lives. Vocational, housing, relationship, physical, or financial changes — all may reduce our *stability* to zero, to put a new slant on the fog report!"[2] Probably everyone has known what it is to journey through life and sud-

212

denly have stability reduced to zero.

Those who have been disappointed too often conclude that no good thing is possible for them. For some, disappointment becomes a habit. It settles into a way of looking at life that asks, "Why try?" The question betrays a bitter and defeated attitude about the world and its prospects.

Professional basketball Hall of Fame member Jerry West recalled his disillusionment upon hearing that his older brother had been killed in combat in the Korean War. "I said, 'That's not true!' and took off running. I ran about a mile to where we lived. It was awful. I can't describe how awful it was." Life changed after that, West recalls. "I became quieter and more introspective after my brother died, and I often turned to basketball as an outlet." He commented on the disappointment that comes from losing a loved one suddenly: "I'm just not sure people understand the devastation it causes families. I know what it did to ours."[3]

Those who suffer great disappointment often wind up feeling alone. *Nobody understands. Nothing ever works out. What's the point?*

It's tempting to secretly nurse the wound of disappointment by harboring resentment, cynicism, and self-pity, quietly resigning from the game of life. Few will take the effort to pierce the cynic's armor. It's possible to live an entire life under the blackened cloud of disappointment.

It's possible. But it's not necessary.

There is hope for those who have drawn life's short straw. God's Word offers a road map that leads from frustration to joy.

GOD'S WORD

Nobody worked harder than Elijah. This irascible prophet was the spiritual dynamo of ancient Israel — the greatest, most colorful, and most fearless of all God's preachers. He dared more, did more, and achieved more than any other prophet before or since. But he carried a secret burden common among people of passion. He was bitterly disappointed that his labor did not produce greater results. You can read his story in 1 Kings 17–21 and 2 Kings 1–2.

Elijah did what few people dare to do — he spoke truth to power. When the wicked King Ahab disobeyed God, Elijah confronted him and declared that there would be a drought in the land. On another occasion, to prove that there is only one true God, he faced down 450 prophets of Baal on Mount Carmel, calling down fire from heaven in an awesome display of God's might. Later, in an exercise of pure faith, he called out to God on behalf of a widow whose only son had died. God raised the boy to life. Elijah's energy and audacity seemed to know no bounds.

But his life was not perfect. Ahab and his notorious wife, Jezebel, hated Elijah and swore to kill him. This evil duo had induced nearly all of the people to turn away from the Lord and worship the false god Baal. Elijah was forced to live in hiding. To escape from the wicked king, Elijah became an outlaw prophet, living on the lam, hiding in ravines or deserted places. On one occasion he nearly starved to death and was saved only by ravens, who carried bread to him.

Finally, Elijah tired of being the lone holdout for God. In spite of his great achievements, Ahab's hold on the people only grew stronger. Tired of living with a price on his head, Elijah made his way into the desert, where he found a cave for shelter. That night, exhausted, frustrated, and disappointed by life, Elijah had a conversation with God.

"What are you doing here, Elijah?"

"I have been very zealous for the Lord," Elijah answered, "And I am the only one left" (1 Kings 19:9–10).

Elijah's response has been echoed by nearly everyone who faces disappointment. *I work hard, but nobody seems to care. There isn't any point in doing right; good people suffer, and wicked people thrive. I've tried and tried and tried — it's just not worth it anymore.*

Elijah had reached the end of his passion. Dejected, depressed, and disappointed with life, he wished to die. There was no plan for suicide — the frustrated prophet simply could not see any point in going on. He succumbed to the temptation common to all for whom life becomes a disappointment: he pitied himself.

But, as He so often does, God crashed the gate at Elijah's pity party. The Father's response to Elijah's pathetic lament forms a lesson for all of the brokenhearted.

We Look for God in the Wrong Places

God told Elijah to go out of the cave and stand in front of the mountain. "I'm going to pass by there in just a minute," God said. "You won't want to miss this." Elijah scampered to the entrance of the cave.

Immediately, a tornado descended from the sky and tore the mountain to pieces. Shattered rock fell in huge chunks all around Elijah. But God was nowhere to be seen. Suddenly there was a mighty earthquake. The ground shook violently, and Elijah was knocked to his knees. But when he looked up, God still wasn't there. Then a fire roared over the land in front of Elijah, destroying all vegetation and scorching the earth. When the smoke cleared, Elijah peered across the horizon. God *still* wasn't there.

If God wasn't in the whirlwind and wasn't in the earthquake and wasn't in the fire, where on earth was He?

Then, as he stood listening and waiting, Elijah heard it. It was a soft voice, a gentle whisper, but there was no mistaking the sound. It was God. Not in the whirlwind, not in the earthquake, not in the fire, but in a still, small voice God spoke to Elijah.

"Here I am," God whispered. "And I've been here all along. Now, tell me again, Elijah — what are you crying about?"

We're disappointed because God has not done what we think He should. Since He didn't show up when we wanted Him to, we figure that He must have abandoned us. We look for great, awesome displays of God's power that provide what we want — right now! But God often chooses to work in subtle ways. When He doesn't conform to our expectations, we're disappointed. But God is always active in our lives. We simply don't see because we're usually looking in the wrong direction. We expect a miracle, but God is teaching us patience. We hope for immediate business success, but God intends for us to be diligent. We hope for romance, but God calls us to self-reliance.

Are the things we long for wrong? No, but they may not be God's agenda at the moment. We're disappointed because we don't get what *we* want. But God may be pursuing an entirely different goal.

What is your greatest disappointment? Could it be that God had some other equally good thing in mind for you? How do you know that God isn't at work even in those things that you see as nothing?

God Knows More than We Do

Elijah felt alone. He believed that he was the only one who had continued to be faithful to God. He concluded that God was doing nothing in the world — because he could see no evidence of it. He couldn't have been more wrong.

Even as Elijah cowered in his cave, God had already identified 7,000 people throughout the land who continued to be faithful. In fact, God was about to launch a major offensive in the spiritual battle for Israel. Elijah just didn't know it yet.

It's always the case that God knows more than we do, does more than we know, and has plans that He chooses not to reveal to us — unless we need to know.

If you've faced some bitter disappointment, who knows — God may already be at work, moving you toward a delightful discovery or joy-filled triumph. Sitting alone in the dark, Elijah had no idea what God was up to. We seldom do either.

God Puts Whiners to Work

Elijah was in such a fit of self-pity that he probably would have chosen to lay in the cave and do nothing. "What's the point?" he whined. "They'll probably kill me along with the rest of the prophets." But God didn't feel the least bit sorry for Elijah. Rather than commiserating with the dejected prophet, He put him to work.

"Go back the way you came," God told Elijah, "and . . . anoint Hazael king over Aram. Also, anoint Jehu son of Nimshi king over Israel, and anoint Elisha son of Shaphat from Abel Meholah to succeed you as prophet" (1 Kings 19:15–16). These instructions showed that God had big plans in the works. There was plenty to do, and the whining prophet had a role to play. Did Elijah expect a few weeks of R and R after all his hard work? Instead of a seven-day pass, he was sent back to the front!

Are you recovering from a bitter disappointment? Rather than wallow in self-pity, think: *What might God have for me to do next?*

We Don't Always See the Results

Elijah was told to appoint his own successor. That meant that Elijah's own work was nearly finished. Elisha became Elijah's assistant at first and then took his place as the great prophet of Israel after Elijah was taken to heaven in a chariot of fire (see 2 Kings 2:11). Elisha continued the work Elijah had begun, going on to achieve great successes of his own.

You may not see the result of your labors, but that is no cause for disappointment. Franklin Roosevelt did not see the end of World War II, but he was no less successful in bringing about its conclusion. You may not see your children come to Christ during your lifetime, but they may honor Him after your death. It may not be you, but your son, who succeeds in the business you're struggling to create.

What is your most recent disappointment? Is it possible that you have witnessed only one battle, not the whole war? You may never see all the results of your labors. God is in control of the world and everything in it. That includes you. You won't see the whole picture; not now, not ever. Can you trust God to win the war, even if you lose a few skirmishes along the way?

Steps to Healing

So where do you go from here? How do you find the courage, as Elijah did, to force yourself out of the cave of disappointment and get back to the business of living? The most difficult step in this recovery is the first one. Overcoming the paralysis that insists, "There's no point in trying again," is the key to healing. Here are some practical things that lead to that all-important first step.

Realize That It's Not About You

Disappointment is a highly personal emotion. When our desires for love, success, or achievement have been frustrated, the world seems to stop. But it doesn't. Often the real causes of our disappointment have nothing to do with ourselves. Sometimes we're just a small part in the much bigger picture.

The CEO who ordered the layoff may have been more concerned about saving 2,000 jobs than cutting 50. The decision wasn't about you. The teacher had a responsibility to help all students succeed. The attention she paid to them was not a slight to you.

Nobody likes to hear that there are more important things in the world than their love life or their finances. Step back and take a wide-angle view of your life. See where you fit into the world and into God's plan. Chances are, there are things going on around you that are even more critical than what you're facing.

Remember What God Has Done

Disappointment absorbs our attention. We get sucked into it like a hole. It dominates our thoughts and emotions for days or weeks, even years. It's easy to become so focused on the few things that have gone wrong that we lose sight of the many things that have gone right.

Yet God has done great things in the past — your past. List them. Write down the good things that God provided for you. Add to the list now and then. Read it once in a while. Never allow your present circumstances to cloud your view of the future or color your memory of the past. God has done great things — *for you.* Celebrate them.

Trust God's Promises

God's promises are not abridged by your circumstances. You may be alarmed by what you're facing, but rest assured: God's plan for the universe continues to move along on schedule. God is up to something big in the world, and He'll continue to make it happen. What He has said He will do. Make a list of the promises God has given in Scripture. Place a check mark beside the ones that apply to you. Have these promises been canceled? Could it be that God has changed His mind?

No way. They're all still true. Trust God to keep His word.

Remember that it took Edison more than a thousand failed experiments to invent the incandescent light. God took thousands of years from the Garden of Eden to bring His saving Son into the world. Rome wasn't built in a day. Should your life be different? Look to the future. Don't judge yourself or the world or God by what's happening at this moment.

Do Something

Don't sit in a lonely cave like Elijah, waiting for something good to happen. Self-pity will waste your strength as surely as a disease. God responded to Elijah's self-pity by assigning work. What does God have for you to do? What is His will for your life? For your family? For your career? For your ministry, serving others?

What have you learned from your experience that will enable you to pursue your work more diligently, more successfully, in the future? What can you do right now, today, that will take your mind off of yourself, open your eyes to the bigger picture, and put you back into action?

Choose to take action. Choose to trust. Choose to believe that the future can be better than the past. Then do something to make it so.

THE POINT OF HEALING

After Dennis and Kim had collected themselves there in the Chicago motel, their disappointment turned to resentment. Angry phone calls to their lawyer were followed by a tense call to Stacie.

"I just want my babies back," Stacie pleaded.

"Think about what you're doing," Dennis demanded. "Think about the boys. You can't do this."

"Yes, I can," Stacie said firmly. "And I'm going to. I want my children. Bring them to the social worker's office in the morning."

Anger gave way to calculated calm as Dennis responded coolly, "No. I'm not baby-sitting your kids all night. If you want them, come get them. Now."

"I was dying inside," Dennis admits. "But I couldn't hold those boys another night and then let them go."

Dreams and delight lay in a heap of disappointment beside the sleeping infants. Like robots, Dennis and Kim gathered up the receiving blankets, tiny stuffed animals, matching clothes — and waited. The taxicab arrived just before midnight. Stacie and a friend climbed out of the backseat, empty-handed. She had brought nothing — no car seat, no blankets, no baby clothes, no bottles, just her determination to take the children. Dennis and Kim each carried one of the boys. They hugged them tenderly, kissed them, and held them together. Then they let them go.

"I was angry," Dennis admits, "but not at Stacie."

"It's weird," Kim recalls. "We weren't mad at her — she was just a kid herself. But we were mad at *everybody* somehow."

The couple spent several months in a kind of haze. "At first I couldn't eat or sleep," Kim says. "But after the shock wore off, I was just angry." The disappointment of losing Nathan and Daniel produced a cynical attitude about life. "We didn't trust anyone. We just wanted the world to go away."

"And we owed all that money," Dennis adds. "We felt used."

Then the phone rang again. The lawyer. Another agency had an adoption opportunity. They were first in line for consideration. "What do you want to do?"

"I knew we had to do it," Dennis recalls. "We wanted children. But to have them, we'd have to trust someone again."

"I knew that trying for another adoption was a risk," Kim says, "but we couldn't live the rest of our lives like that, in a prison of self-pity. We had to get out."

They said yes, and this time there was no disappointment. A few months later, Kim and Dennis welcomed a son, Adam, into their home. And there would be more sons. Three years later, another adoption opportunity came their way.

"I'm on my way to the hospital," Kim said in the familiar call to Dennis's office. Half an hour later, they met in the childbirth unit where a smiling social worker gave evidence that God is gracious. "It's twins," she said. "Twin boys. Somehow that wasn't noticed during the prenatal exam. I hope you'll be able to take them both."

"Yes!" They said it together.

"There's more," the social worker said cautiously. "There's a minor problem. One of the boys is not breathing well. He should be fine, but he's fighting an infection right now. You need to know that he's ill."

"That doesn't matter," Dennis said, speaking for both of them. "He's our son, no matter what. Some things you just have to take on faith."

Your Journey

Exploring Your Story

1. What has been your greatest disappointment with life? Share that story with someone.

2. How do you tend to respond to disappointments? With anger? Self-pity? Resentment? All of the above?

3. Draw a line chart that shows the victories and disappointments that you've experienced in life. Label each peak and valley, and show where you are today.

Exploring God's Word

1. Read Elijah's encounter with God in 1 Kings 19:9–18.

2. List the reasons that Elijah had for feeling disappointed with life.

3. From a psychological standpoint, de-

scribe the approach that God took in dealing with Elijah. Do you think this approach was successful? What other approaches might God have used to communicate with Elijah?

Exploring the Steps to Healing

1. Make a list of the things you've been putting off doing because you've suffered disappointment or have feared failure. Choose one thing, and tell when you will begin to do it.

2. Interview someone you know who has suffered a great disappointment in life, perhaps someone who suffered a business failure or a broken engagement. Ask that person how God helped him or her to recover from that disappointment. Then share with a friend what you learned.

3. Spend some time in prayer, asking God this question: *Lord, what do You want me to do next?*

AFTERWORD

This book has been a journal of sorts, recording the everyday struggles of real people. They represent thousands of others, people in your community, your church, or even your family — people just like you. We have pledged to protect their privacy. In return, they have exposed their innermost feelings in the pages of this book — their pain, their selfishness, their doubts and fears, and ultimately their pathway to healing.

As we talked with these and other veterans of spiritual combat, we noticed a common theme. Nearly all of them had felt anger in some form or other. They were variously frustrated by their own shortcomings, exasperated at their physical limitations, furious at the villainy of others, and bitter toward God. Through the lens of their experience, this fact became clear: *Anger is the universal response to pain. We hate it that life isn't fair.*

These everyday heroes had something else in common.

They shared a trait that led to their recovery, and that was *a willingness to trust God.* Those who grieved determined to hope in the future. Those who suffered physically learned dependence. Those who had been betrayed came to forgive. In each case, the basis of their resignation was faith: they trusted the promises of God enough to act on them. Their acceptance of life's circumstances was rooted in confidence that God could — and would — redeem their suffering.

For you who may now be discovering the painful truth that life doesn't always turn out as you had planned, we believe those common themes will also apply. Life is remarkably predictable in that it disappoints each of us sooner or later. And that disappointment produces anger — at others, at life, at God. The question, then, is not whether your life will be perfect — it won't be. It's whether you'll hold on to faith in spite of what you suffer. Will you, like Laura Johnson, learn to treasure the past but look to the future? Or, like Janet Forsythe, will you surrender your anger in spite of your hurt? Will you, like Mark Evans, call out to

God in your lowest moment rather than accuse Him?

It's not impossible. These nine and countless others have done that — believed God in spite of what they saw, felt, or experienced. Paul asks, "If God is for us, who can be against us?" (Rom. 8:31). Who indeed? No circumstance is beyond His power to redeem. No matter where you are in your journey, you're not at the end of the road. Life may have gone horribly wrong, but God's design for you is not defeat.

Listen.

When they found Lauren Calhoun, locked in the lice-infested closet of a mobile home in Dallas, she was so ill and emaciated that neighbors said she didn't look human. The eight-year-old girl had been imprisoned in a closet or small room off and on for more than three years by a fanatically abusive mother. Physically abused, neglected, left naked, and nearly starved, she weighed only 25 pounds and stood just three feet tall when she was rescued. She had lived in the dark for more than four months.

But she was not alone.

Voices from the radio had become friends to her. The loud music had been intended to mask her pathetic cries for help. Instead, the lyrics of popular songs became her hope of escaping an abusive home. As she listened to songs about love and acceptance, she dreamed that someday someone would love her too. Abandoned, abused, nearly too weak to sit up, all she could do was listen to the music.

The neighbor who found Lauren opened a window of heaven, reached into hell, and set her free. She lives now with her adoptive parents, Bill and Sabrina Kavanaugh, and her life is returning to normal. "With the exception of her size," Bill says, "to look at her you'd never know [what] she went through."[1]

The enemy laughed as music blared through the thin walls of that mobile home. But the King of Kings had the last word, using those same raucous sounds to speak His peace to a troubled heart.

He'll do that for you too.

Right now He's playing a medley of grace for an audience of one lonely soul trapped in a closet of doubt and fear. Listen, and you'll hear the words of His song in every scripture, every sunrise, every word of hope offered by a friend, even in your own heart. No matter what circumstances now conspire to make your life appear hopeless, these grace notes still echo through the thin walls of time — you are forgiven, you are loved, and you are free.

Never stop listening to that music.

NOTES

Chapter 1

1. Maria Hong, *Family Abuse: A National Epidemic* (Springfield, N.J.: Enslow Publishers, 1997), 8.
2. Dale Robert Reinert, *Sexual Abuse and Incest* (Springfield, N.J.: Enslow Publishers, 1997), 57.
3. Ibid., 47.

Chapter 2

1. Corrie ten Boom, "When We Can't, God Can," *Decision,* May 1992, 34.

Chapter 5

1. Mark A. Reinecke (March 28, 2003), "Are You Suffering from War-Induced Anxiety?" <www.msnbc.com>.
2. From Henry F. Lyte's hymn "Praise, My Soul, the King of Heaven."
3. Norman G. Wilson and Jerry Brecheisen, *The Call to Contentment: Life Lessons from*

the Beatitudes (Indianapolis: Wesleyan Publishing House, 2002), 44.

Chapter 6

1. Natalie Fazzin (January 7, 2003), "Study Links Chronic Pain to Signals in the Brain," National Institute of Neurological Disorders and Stroke web site, <www.ninds.nih.gov>.

2. Oregon State University Health and Science (2003), "Chronic Pain: What Is Pain?" under Health Topics: Spine, Shoulder, and Pelvis, <www.ohsuhealth.com>.

3. Ibid.

4. Associated Press (May 9, 2002), "Geriatrics Society Gives Hints to Fight Off Pain," <www.usatoday.com>.

5. Carl T. Hall (November 4, 2002), "Social Factors May Deepen Chronic Pain: Scientists Go Beyond Physical Causes," *San Francisco Chronicle,* on-line ed., <www.sfgate.com>.

6. W. Reed Moran (February 8, 2001), "Gymnast Bart Conner Aces Arthritis," <www.usatoday.com>.

7. Nicole Winfield (April 5, 2003), "Saving Pfc. Lynch: Central Command Releases Details of Rescue," <www.indystar.com>.

Chapter 7

1. "Cassia Eller, 39, Was Brazilian Rock Star," *Indianapolis Star,* December 31, 2001, B4.
2. Associated Press (February 7, 2003), "Man Confesses in Ad, Faces Charges," <www.newsday.com>.

Chapter 8

1. Lewis E. Kraus, Susan Stoddard, and David Gilmartin, *Chartbook on Disability in the United States, 1996* (report prepared for United States Department of Education, #H133D50017, National Institute on Disability and Rehabilitation Research, Washington, D.C., by InfoUse, Berkeley, Calif., 1996), 5.
2. "Thoughts on Positive Living," *Inspiration University,* vol. 3, issue 7 (December 14, 2001). <www.angelfire.com/nv/inspirationuniv/volume3/issue7/htm>

Chapter 9

1. Charisma News Service (December 16, 2002), "Worship Leader Shares God's Heart Despite 'Limp,' " *New Man,* on-line ed., <www.newmanmag.com>.
2. Stan A. Toler, *The Buzzards Are Circling, but God's Not Finished with Me Yet* (Tulsa, Okla.: RiverOak Publishing, 2001), 25.

3. Mark Montieth, "War Death Took Heavy Toll," *Indianapolis Star,* April 6, 2003, C7.

Afterword

1. Jennifer Emily, "Texas Girl Who Was Confined in Closet Begins a New Life," *Indianapolis Star,* July 18, 2002, A7; and Steve McGonigle and Jennifer Emily, "Mother gave daughter up for adoption, won her back; Pair accused of keeping girl in closet are remorseful," *The Dallas Morning News,* on-line ed., June 14, 2001 <dallasnews.com>.